PURITY UNDER pressuRe

NEIL T. ANDERSON AND DAVE PARK

HARVEST HOUSE PUBLISHERS
Eugene, Oregon 97402

Interior art by Scott Angle

Cover by Garborg Design Works, Minneapolis, Minneasota

PURITY UNDER PRESSURE

Copyright © 1995 by Harvest House Publishers
Eugene, Oregon 97402

Library of Congress Cataloging-in-Publication Data

Anderson, Neil T., 1942–
    Purity under pressure / Neil T. Anderson and Dave Park.
        p. cm.
    ISBN 1-56507-292-8
    1. Chastity/Religious—Juvenile literature. 2. Teenagers—Religion life.
3. Teenagers—Conduct of life. 4. Teenagers—Sexual behavior—
Juvenile literature. 5. Christian life—Juvenile literature.
I. Park, David, 1961–   . II. Title.
BV4647.C5A56   1995   95-14443
241'.66—dc20   CIP

Printed in the United States of America.

01 / BC / 10 9 8 7 6

This book is dedicated to all those who would love to retain their sexual purity and to all those who would like to be free again in Christ. May you stand firm when your purity is under pressure.

Acknowledgments

What a team God has given us. Who could have dreamed that God, in such a short time, would raise up such a wonderful youth ministry? Thank you so much for caring enough for young people to cry with them, laugh with them, and plan for their freedom. You all work too hard, sleep too little, and get paid too late (heaven). Roger and Debby McNichols, Rich and Shirley Miller, Jim and Donna Wern, Larry and Joyce Beckner, Dawson and Karen Grover, Dan and Tammy Roelofs, Nancy Wilson and Tuggy Dunton—you are the best. Thank you for all your hard work and support.

Thank you to the whole crew at Harvest House, with a special thanks to Barb Sherrill and Gloria Kempton.

A special thanks to our wonderful wives, Joanne and Grace, who were worth waiting for.

—Neil and Dave

Contents

1. Who You Are.............................   7

Part One: Relationships and Purity

2. Picking Your Peers 23
3. Dating in 3D 39
4. Am I Really in Love? 55

Part Two: God's Design and Purity

5. God's View on Sex 75
6. Why God Says Wait 91
7. Detecting the Dangers in a Sex-Crazed World.. 105
8. Pathways to a Dead End 117
9. The Seduction of Your Mind 131

Part Three: Freedom and Purity

10. How a Habit Forms....................... 145
11. You're Alive!............................ 157
12. Choosing to Believe the Truth.............. 175
13. Steps to Freedom in Christ 193
14. Living Free and Staying Free 229

> *Don't let anyone look down on you because you are young, but set an example for the believers in speech, in life, in love, in faith, and in purity.*
> *1 Timothy 4:12*

CHAPTER ONE

Who You Are

The Bible plainly indicates that certain conditions will prevail just before the end. For example, the prophet Daniel said "even to the time of the end . . . knowledge shall be increased" (Daniel 12:4 KJV). Today there is more knowledge about everything than at any other time in history. I read recently that 90 percent of all the world scientists and engineers who have ever lived are alive today. Our high schools, colleges, and universities are turning out 4 million graduates every year. But although our young people are gaining knowledge, they are not always acquiring wisdom to use that knowledge.

—Billy Graham [1]

You live in a dangerous world. Every day you're faced with choices that can affect the rest of your life—choices about relationships, friendships, and dating. You face all kinds of sexual pressure and peer pressure—each one pulling at your purity. How can you hold on to your purity in a world that constantly mocks it?

The Big Picture

A flood of sex education courses have been created to stop the increase in teen pregnancy. In the past 20 years Christian leaders have given the church hundreds of seminars, books, tapes, and videos on the subject. How are we doing? Have our efforts worked? Has all of that information and education stopped sexual promiscuity in your peer group? Since 1970, teen pregnancy among 15- to 19-year-olds has gone up 32 percent.[2] Knowing what the Bible teaches is a must. But it's not enough to simply know the dos and don'ts about sex and relationships. The knowledge is not enough to empower you to do what's right.

We in the body of Christ have yet to address the whole issue. We too often attack the problem of sexual promiscuity as if all we need to do is try to help you keep your hormones in check. Certainly, we must deal with the physical side of sexuality, but what about the spiritual side? And what about relationships? In addition to arming you with the latest facts about AIDS, sexually transmitted diseases, and the abstinence message, we must also teach you about temptation and the true nature of the tempter. We must talk about confession and renunciation. The fact is that pride, rebellion, unforgiveness, false religions, and the sins of our parents can all open the door to sexual problems as much as can physical sex drives. Whom you pick for friends and the relationships you develop will have an influence on your sexual purity. You are not just facing one enemy—you're up against three. The Bible calls them the world, the flesh, and the devil.

Three Enemies

All three of these enemies play a part in temptation, and we must arm ourselves to win the battle for purity in each area. The world and the flesh are not the only battle fronts, as it often seems. The devil and his "spiritual forces of evil" (Ephesians 6:12) are at work introducing evil suggestions into your mind. "The Spirit clearly says that in later times some will abandon the faith and follow deceiving spirits and things taught by demons (1 Timothy 4:1). Just as we learn to deal with worldly and fleshly influences, so we must learn to distinguish Satan's subtle, personal influence and resist him. We need to see the big picture. Of course, not every evil thought that enters our mind is the voice of Satan or a demon. The flesh—that part of us that wants to live selfishly and independent of God—also comes up with sinful thoughts and evil deeds. Input from movies, music, books, TV, and other media also introduces evil ideas into our minds at times. As we grow in Christ, we learn how to say no to the deeds of the flesh, and we learn how to walk in the Spirit. Wherever your evil thoughts are coming from—the world, the flesh, or the devil—this book will help you bring "captive every thought to make it obedient to Christ" (2 Corinthians 10:5).

We know our world and culture are changing, but sometimes we lose sight of just how much. On June 14, 1954, *Life Magazine* reported on a new American ritual "Going Steady." This youth activity raised some eyebrows at the time. But now, according to the Center for Disease Control and Prevention, "Seventy-two percent of American high school seniors have engaged in sex."[3]

This is the world you live in; this is where God has called you to live out purity. It's not going to be easy! When we surveyed almost 1300 Christian high school students, we found that over 70 percent felt that Christianity worked for others but not for them. Unless you understand what the Bible teaches about Satan's strategies, you can easily get stuck in a Romans 7:15 lifestyle: The very thing you *don't want to do*, you *do*; and the very thing you desperately *want to do*, you *don't*. You blame yourself for your defeat and sink into a deep sense of hopelessness and guilt. What can you do in the face of this attack on your purity?

In the Face of Attack

First, you must understand that as a Christian you are not immune to Satan's attack. Why else would Paul tell you to put on the full armor of God? Second, you have hope. Christ's death and resurrection defeated Satan. The war over your purity is a winnable war. Now is the time to learn about your authority and position in Christ, so that you might claim the victory that is yours in Christ Jesus. Romans 12:1,2 urges you, "in view of God's mercy, to offer your bodies as living sacrifices, holy and pleasing to God—which is your spiritual act of worship. Do not conform any longer to the pattern of this world, but be transformed by the renewing of your mind. Then you will be able to test and approve what God's will is—his good, pleasing and perfect will."

Some Important Background

God cares about our relationships, and He is especially concerned about our relationship with Him. In Genesis 2:7 we read how God made man and "breathed into his nostrils the breath of life; and man became a living being." God created man so that He could have an intimate friendship with him. To have that friendship, Adam was created alive in two ways: First, he was alive physically; second, he was alive spiritually. But then Adam and Eve blew it and disobeyed God. As a result, their relationship with God was severed.

Genesis 2:16,17 says, "And the LORD God commanded the man, saying, 'You are free to eat from any tree in the garden; but you must not eat from the tree of the knowledge of good and evil, for when you eat of it you will surely die.' " Well, Adam disobeyed God, and he ate from the tree. Did Adam and Eve physically drop dead? No, but they did start the physical process of dying. The real blow actually occurred spiritually and caused a separation between mankind and God.

Since that time, everyone born into this world is physically alive, but spiritually dead, separated from God. Before coming to Christ, we don't have the presence of God in our lives or any knowledge of His ways, so we lack the ability to live a pure (righteous) life. We have learned to live without Him.

Ephesians 2:1 says, "As for you, you were dead in your transgressions and sins." What does it mean that we were dead? Were we dead physically? Of course not. But we were dead spiritually; we were separated from God.

Jesus came to remove that separation and put us back together with God. He said in John 10:10, "I have come that they may have life, and have it to the full." Eternal life isn't something you receive when you die; it's something you receive the moment you accept Christ. First John 5:11,12 says, "And this is the testimony: God has given us eternal life, and this life is in his Son. He who has the Son has life; he who does not have the Son of God does not have life." As a Christian, you are alive in Christ right now. To be alive means that your soul is in union with God. In the Bible you will see over and over again the truth that you are in Christ or that Christ is in you. It is this life or union with God that gives you your real identity and allows you to live a pure life, even under pressure.

Who Are You?

When asked to describe themselves, most people usually mention race, religion, cultural or family background. But Paul said none of those apply anymore (Colossians 3:10,11) because our identity is no longer determined by our physical heritage, social standing, or race. Our identity lies in the fact that we are all children of God, spiritually alive in Christ.

Every true believer is adopted into the family of God. My (Dave's) brother-in-law, Matthew DuPeire, knows all about adoption. At one time, he had no sense of family and no intimate relationships; all he had was himself and two younger sisters.

As a young boy, Matthew was called Michael. Every day he waddled down the hallway of the shabby old San Linda Hotel, begging for food. The old hotel had a reputation for trouble and was no place for a little boy. Michael was responsible for finding food and caring for his two sisters. He never knew who his father was. He had no notion of what family meant at all. He only knew he had to find food or they would all go hungry. Michael and his sisters were being physically abused, and after countless days and nights of despair, Michael cried out to God, "I don't know what Your name is, or who You are, but I need You. Help me, please help me." The next day someone told a local pastor about the three orphan children abandoned by their mother at a hotel. The pastor took the young children in until they could be adopted. Michael was adopted by my father-and mother-in-law.

Michael became Matthew; he received a whole new identity and family, a new name, new relationships, new everything. The same was true for him spiritually; Matt had received Christ as his personal Savior and was also adopted into the family of God. Because of his relationship with Christ, he received a new spiritual identity. He was no longer lost in his sins because he had received Christ and His righteousness. Matt will never doubt the fact of his adoption into the DuPeire family. The changes from the old home to the new home were drastic. In the same way we need to understand who we are in Christ and our new identity in Him.

Just like Matt, many of us have experienced rejection, abandonment, and abuse. Even those who have had a fairly good childhood have been victimized in some way by the enemy's subtle deceptions. If we're not careful those experiences can affect our belief system and cause an attitude that says, "I'm not worth anything. I'm no good. I can't do anything right. Nobody loves me. Nobody cares."

Without exception, all the young people with whom we have counseled have had some unbiblical belief that the enemy has used against them. Jesus said in John

8:32, "Then you will know the truth, and the truth will set you free." We must learn to recognize faulty beliefs from our past, renounce them, and then renew our minds with God's truth.

Although I am sure Matt is thankful for his new family, I'm confident he is far more grateful for his new relationship with Christ; he has been given a new life in Christ, gained forgiveness for his sins, received the Holy Spirit, and has become a partaker "of the divine nature, having escaped the corruption that is in the world by lust" (2 Peter 1:4 NASB).

A Christian's deepest identity is that of a saint, a child born of God, a divine masterpiece, a child of light, and a citizen of heaven.

> But you are a chosen people, a royal priesthood, a holy nation, a people belonging to God, that you may declare the praises of Him who called you out of darkness into his wonderful light. Once you were not a people, but now you are the people of God; once you had not received mercy, but now you have received mercy (1 Peter 2:9,10).

Second Corinthians 5:17 says, "Therefore if anyone is in Christ, he is a new creation; the old has gone, the new has come!"

Learning Who You Are

When we were dead in our trespasses and sins, we learned to live our lives without God. Our identity and how we viewed ourselves was programmed into us from our fallen world and our relationships with others. But our past or our sexual sins no longer determine who we are. Now, Christ's work on the cross determines our identity.

Renewing our minds doesn't come naturally; there is no automatic "clear button" that erases our past programming. We must consciously know the Word of God so we can understand who we are from God's point of view. Who are you? First John 3:1-3 says,

> How great is the love the Father has lavished on us, that we should be called children of God! And that is what we are! The reason the world does not know us is that it did not know him. Dear friends, now we are children of God, and what we will be has not yet been made known. But we know that when he appears, we shall be like him, for we shall see him as he is. Everyone who has this hope in him purifies himself, just as he is pure.

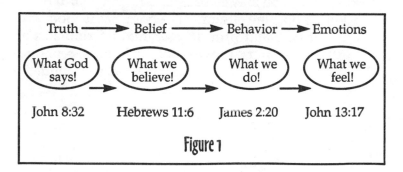

Figure 1

The most important belief we can have is a true knowledge of who God is. The second most important belief is to know the truth about who we are as children of God, because we can't continually behave in a way that is different from how we view ourselves. If we fail to see ourselves as God sees us, then we will suffer from a wrong identity and a poor image of who we really are.

It is not what we do that determines who we are. It is who we are that determines what we do (see Figure 1).

Somebody Doesn't Want You to Know

It's easy to forget who we are in Christ. Why? Because Satan doesn't want us to be free. If you want to know more about who you are in Christ, we strongly recommend you read *Stomping Out the Darkness* and *The Bondage Breaker* (Youth Edition) to prepare for this book. How do we live each day with an awareness of who we are as children of God, so that we can walk in fellowship with Him? First, by reading God's Word, and secondly by fellowshipping with God and other Christians.

As you read, be aware that Satan does not want you to know this. You may actually struggle in your thought life with opposing arguments about what God says about purity. Stand firm. If your mind formulates an idea that is contrary to what the Bible says, renounce the lie and accept God's truth. If possible, say aloud, "In Jesus' name, get!" One young girl wrote:

Dear Neil and Dave,

I'm writing to you to tell you how much I enjoyed your book *The Bondage Breaker* (Youth Edition). It has really helped me break the bondage with Satan. Before I read the book I was trapped in a sin that kept repeating itself. I'd confess and it would come back a few

> days later. It was a vicious cycle. Now when
> Satan tempts me with that sin, I just do what
> you said to do. I say out loud, "In the name of
> Jesus Christ, Satan and everything evil here,
> leave now." It works *every* time! I'm so proud
> that I finally broke free. Thank you so much!
> I'm 15 years old and if you helped me I'm
> sure you'll help many other teens too! Thanks
> again.

This book was written to help you avoid the traps
that the world and Satan may throw at you, and to free
you if sexual bondage is robbing you of your victory in
Christ. We don't want anything hindering your maturity in Christ. We are offering no magic formulas. Rather,
we want to point you to the truth of God's Word regarding sexual temptation, sexual bondage, Satan's destructive role in the struggle, your identity in Christ, and
God's provision for your freedom. Also, in chapter 13,
the Steps to Freedom in Christ will guide you as you
renounce behaviors and false beliefs which have kept
you in bondage. They will help you to receive the freedom which is your inheritance in Christ.

Part One of this book identifies the importance of
friendships, dating, and relationships that last as they
relate to who you are in Christ. You will learn how to
establish godly relationships.

Part Two centers on what the Bible says about sex
and why God says to wait on sex until marriage—the
abstinence message.

Part Three shows the way of escape from sexual
temptation and bondage which Jesus Christ has provided for us. You will learn what you need to believe
and what you need to do to secure your freedom in

Christ. You will discover how to win the battle over sexual temptation in your mind.

This book is also for those who have been sexually exploited through the act of rape, incest, molestation, or any other kind of abuse. Most of the teenagers who come to Freedom In Christ Ministries for help can trace their problems to some kind of sexual abuse. We want to show how the gospel can put an end to victimization and stop the cycle of abuse. We believe that Christ is the only answer, and that the truth can set both the victim and the perpetrator free.

It is our prayer that you will find the freedom Jesus Christ purchased for you on the cross. If you're trapped by the shackles of sexual sin, you can find freedom if you will throw yourself upon the mercy of God. Freedom comes through "Christ in you, the hope of glory" (Colossians 1:27). Jesus Christ can and will help you when your purity is under pressure.

Purity Pointers

Read: Review each of the Scriptures given in Figure 1. Now read Ephesians 1.

Reflect: 1. How often do you see the phrase "in Christ" or "in Him" in the first chapter of Ephesians? What did you think as you read those phrases about you?

2. Do you and Jesus say the same things and believe the same thing about who you are? What are the differences?

3. Have you accepted Jesus' truth about who

you are in Christ? Or are you getting your identity from another source?

4. Do you ever feel like your past behavior or your sexual sins determine who you are? Why does Christ's work on the cross determine your identity?

Respond: My dear heavenly Father, I'm so thankful that I can call on You because I now know that I am Your child. Thank You for sending Jesus to die in my place for my sins so that I may have a new life in Christ. Thank You for the hope that I now have for living a free and pure life because of Christ within me. I renounce the lies of Satan that would rob me of my victory and identity in Christ. I choose to believe who I am in Christ because I have received You into my life by faith. I now commit myself to renew my mind according to the truth of Your Word. In Jesus' name I pray. Amen.

"The Spirit himself testifies with our spirit that we are God's children" (Romans 8:16). Are you believing what God says about you or are you believing the enemy? Let Him reveal to you the lies you may be believing. Check each one that identifies how you think.

❑ Sometimes how I look is more important to me than accepting how God made me.
❑ Sometimes I look to my accomplishments in life to meet my need for significance.

❑ I often don't feel good about who I am.
❑ I often feel insecure around my friends, like my life doesn't even count.
❑ Sometimes I put other people down so my friends will think I'm better than others.
❑ I feel like I've sinned so much that I can never be made holy.
❑ I feel like nobody loves and accepts me, not even God.
❑ I admit that I have not believed what God has said about me.

Lord, I confess that I have not believed what You have said about me by_____.
Thank You for forgiving me and promising that You will never leave me. In Jesus' name I pray. Amen.

—— P A R T O N E ——

Relationships
and
Purity

> *He who loves a pure heart and whose speech is*
> *gracious will have the king for his friend.*
> Proverbs 22:11

—CHAPTER TWO—

Picking Your Peers

> The source of a teen's security is usually
> found in his acceptance by others—especially
> his peers. The affirmation of one's self-worth,
> humanly speaking, is rooted in the opinions
> of others. When there is an overriding need
> for affirmation, a teen will become vulnerable
> to peer pressure.
>
> —Josh McDowell[1]

We all need affirmation, love, and acceptance.
Family and friends are important, and we need their
guidance and care. But nothing can compare nor
replace what Christ alone provides in terms of security,
significance, and meaning.

If you understand who you are in Christ, if you
know your identity is found "in Him," it's far easier to

stand against any kind of pressure. But if your identity is coming from a source other than Christ, it is only a matter of time before the world, the flesh, or the devil pressure you into compromising what you know is right.

When it comes to purity, our foundation must be a rock solid understanding of who we are in Christ. Then we must build upon that foundation by establishing godly friendships. Your friendships are one of the strongest guiding forces in your life, either a force for good or a force for evil.

What Is a True Friend?

Several years ago a young man entered my (Neil's) college ministry like a storm. It was the most incredible song-and-dance routine I had ever seen. If you looked in the dictionary under "extrovert," it would probably say, "see Danny." For about a month, he showed off his sharp wit and fun-loving nature. Then one day he came to my office deeply depressed and asked me, "Why don't I have any friends?"

I looked at him and said, "I think it's because we don't know who you really are. You come across as this funny guy, but deep down you are hurting, aren't you?" I told him I thought I could be his friend if I got to know him.

True friendships involve loyalty, devotion, and support. Without godly friendships, loneliness is bound to creep into your life.

A true friendship is two-sided; both people share and give of themselves. For a true friendship to take place you must see yourself as a child of God and see the other person as someone created in the image of God as well. Otherwise you just become acquaintances and never companions. At our conferences, we often ask the question, "In the short time we are together, if we really got to know you, would we like you?" Then we always respond, "I'm sure we would." Without exception, this is true of the people we have come to know intimately, even if they have trouble relating socially or are afraid of getting close to others. After hearing about the difficulties in their pasts, we find that as a result of knowing them, we come to enjoy them and love them.

Developing friendships is risky. You have to open yourself up to others and be real! It's true no one person apart from Christ can meet all our emotional needs, but without taking the risk and opening up to a trusted friend you never develop the intimacy you so desperately want and need.

What Is Real?

In the story of the *Velveteen Rabbit* by Margery Williams, the little rabbit learns what it means to be real from the old skin horse.

> The Skin Horse had lived longer in the nursery than any of the others. He was so old that his brown coat was bald in patches and showed the seams underneath, and most of the hairs in his tail had been pulled out to string bead necklaces. He was wise, for he had seen a long succession of mechanical toys arrive to boast and swagger, and by-and-by break their mainsprings and pass away, and he knew that they were only toys, and would never turn into anything else. For nursery magic is strange and wonderful, and only those playthings that are old and wise and

experienced like the Skin Horse understand all about it.

"What is REAL?" asked the Rabbit one day, while they were lying side by side near the nursery fender, before Nana came to tidy the room. "Does it mean having things that buzz inside you and a stick-out?"

"Real isn't how you are made," said the Skin Horse, "it's a thing that happens to you. When a child loves you for a long-long time, not just to play with, but REALLY loves you, then you become Real."

"Does it hurt?" asked the Rabbit.

"Sometimes," said the Skin Horse, for he was always truthful. "When you are Real you don't mind being hurt."

"Does it happen all at once, like being wound up," he asked, "or bit by bit?"

"It doesn't happen all at once," said the Skin Horse. "You become. It takes a long time. That's why it doesn't often happen to people who break easily, or have sharp edges, or who have to be carefully kept. Generally, by the time you are Real, most of your hair has been loved off, and your eyes drop out and you get loose in the joints and very shabby. But these things don't matter at all, because once you are Real you can't be ugly, except to people who don't understand."

"I suppose you are Real?" said the Rabbit. And then he wished he had not said it, for he thought the Skin Horse might be sensitive. But the Skin Horse only smiled.

"The Boy's Uncle made me Real," he said.

"That was a great many years ago; but once you are Real you can't become unreal again. It lasts for always."[2]

In Christ you can become real because you are unconditionally loved and accepted. Once you are real you will never want to become unreal again!

Becoming a Real Friend

Freedom and responsibility go hand in hand. One of the most important responsibilities we have as believers is the proper selection of our friends. There is no better way to enhance your walk of freedom than to select sound friendships. If you select poor friends, trouble is usually not too far away. Proverbs 12:26 says, "A righteous man is cautious in friendship, but the way of the wicked leads them astray."

God wants us to focus on developing our own character while seeking to meet the needs of those around us. "Do nothing out of selfish ambition or vain conceit, but in humility consider others better than yourselves. Each of you should look not only to your own interests, but also to the interests of others. Your attitude should be the same as that of Christ Jesus" (Philippians 2:3-5). This is the way to develop a godly friendship.

1. A Real Friend Will Communicate

Communication can be tricky. As the old saying goes, "I know you believe you understand what I think I said, but I'm not sure you realize that what you heard is not what I meant."

In casual friendships, stage 1, you talk but you really

don't say much. You haven't built up any trust, so you're careful about what you share. You have surface conversation like, "How are you? Did you hear the new Steven Curtis Chapman CD?" and so on. Stage 2 is cliché communication. You talk about others, what they did or said, but not much about you. If you do talk about yourself, it's usually only to relate what you did or said. You're not about to tell the other person your deepest fears or secret struggle. Stage 3 is close communication, and it involves revealing to others how you really feel about something—your true opinions, hopes, fears, needs, and secrets.

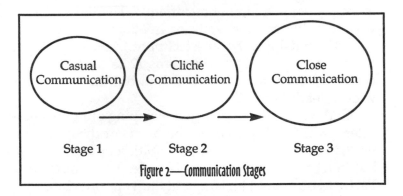

Figure 2—Communication Stages

2. A Real Friend Is Compatible

You can only be a real friend to someone with whom you're compatible. You usually form friendships with those you get along with well and with whom you have something in common. You like to do the same things and you have similar goals and desires. The first place to look for compatibility is in the area of beliefs. Compatibility in beliefs means that not only are you both Christians, but you have the same convictions.

Your friends will influence your belief system either for the good or the bad. The question you need to ask is, do I want to become like that person? "Do not be misled: 'Bad company corrupts good character'" (1 Corinthians 15:33).

3. A Real Friend Develops Others

As a true friend, you must focus on loving and developing others. As you do, you will find that you're also developing yourself. As a Christian friend, you are called to help others grow in their love and walk with Jesus. That makes you a developer. In photography a developer uses chemicals to make a picture on unexposed film become visible. Your job as a Christian developer is similar. You're called to help others see themselves in Christ and grow in their walk of freedom with Him. Like the unexposed film with the picture already on it, it's just waiting to be developed. So, too, you and your Christian friends are just waiting to be developed.

Take a look at your friendships. Do you have your interests at heart or the other person's? Many guys become friends with girls to attempt a sexual conquest. What's your motivation? Is it sexual or is it to develop godly character? Can you be the kind of friend who will stand by others in their lowest moments? And if God gives you the opportunity, are you willing to sacrifice yourself to help meet others' needs? Proverbs 17:17 reminds us, "A friend loves at all times." Jesus loves you all the time—that's why He's the ultimate developer.

4. A Real Friend Accepts Others

Romans 15:7 says, "Accept one another, then, just as

Christ accepted you, in order to bring praise to God." If you can't accept your friends for who they are, you will always be trying to change them, and that is the Holy Spirit's job. We are to accept others just as they are.

A friendship can't withstand the pressures of unacceptance. Without true acceptance it's only a matter of time before the relationship will crumble. Accepting others, of course, doesn't mean you go along with them if they are sinning. You are never called to compromise your character. Jesus loved and accepted sinners but never sinned. He never compromised and changed what He believed or how He behaved.

5. A Real Friend Is Trustworthy

A true friendship is characterized by its degree of trust and loyalty. When someone opens up and tells you a deeply personal feeling or event, what do you do with it? Trustworthiness means keeping a confidence and not using the information others share with you against them. Our friends need to know that they're safe with us, that we won't broadcast their thoughts and feelings all over town. "A perverse man stirs up dissension, and a gossip separates close friends" (Proverbs 16:28). In our youth leadership conferences we often ask people who they would be willing to share their deepest, darkest secret with. Then we ask them to write down the positive character traits of that person. On most everyone's list of qualities is the word "trustworthy" and who they usually end up describing is God.

6. A Real Friend Is an Encourager

A true friend is one who will lead and counsel others in the ways of the Lord. Proverbs 27:9 says, "Oil and perfume make the heart glad, so a man's counsel is sweet to his friend" (NASB). Ask God for the wisdom to know how to listen and empathize with others. As a godly friend, you can learn the art of seeing things from God's point of view. You want to learn how to hang onto biblical truth in the midst of bad circumstances.

Be a friend who will lift and encourage others—one who will laugh with them and cry with them. Be the kind of friend who knows when to offer helpful words of advice and when to be present, but silent.

7. A Real Friend Sacrifices for Others

Jesus said, "For even the Son of Man did not come to be served, but to serve, and to give his life as a ransom for many" (Mark 10:45). Satan doesn't really believe we are capable of living the self-sacrificing life. He believes we are all basically selfish and interested only in what pleases us.

Our new life in Christ, however, makes it possible for us to enter into the kind of servant-oriented life that Christ lived out before us. Jesus calls us to follow His example, but too often we only want what we can get out of a friendship. A true friend may be called upon to sacrifice money and something even more valuable— time. Often the value of something is determined by what it costs you. God invested everything to have a friendship with you. It cost Him His Son! "My command is this: Love each other as I have loved you. Greater love has no one than this, that he lay down his life for his friends" (John 15:12,13).

8. A Real Friend Strengthens Others

True friends help others live out a positive Christian witness and testimony. Proverbs 27:17 says, "As iron sharpens iron, so one man sharpens another." Jesus sent His disciples out two by two for just this reason. Not that we should become Christian snobs, but our closest friends should be believers. We are to always reach out to the lost (Acts 1:8), but those who haven't accepted Christ as their Savior don't possess the Holy Spirit and can only imitate love. James 4:4 reminds us, ". . . don't you know that friendship with the world is hatred toward God? Anyone who chooses to be a friend of the world becomes an enemy of God." True love comes from God and can only be displayed in fullness by one whom the Spirit of God indwells.

We can be a source of strength to others through prayer and loving support. We are not, however, called to compromise our beliefs or our behavior to satisfy our friends; we are even called to avoid bad company (Proverbs 1:8-18).

9. A Real Friend Is Honest with Others

Satan by his very nature is a liar. He would love it if all of your relationships with your friends were riddled with deceptions and lies. Ephesians 4:15 says, "Instead, speaking the truth in love, we will in all things grow up into him who is the Head, that is, Christ." Learn how to share your true feelings and thoughts. We're often afraid to tell others what we really believe because we fear ridicule. But if your friends can't accept you and your beliefs, then they really aren't your friends. True friendship and understanding comes on the coattails of honesty. Can you share who you are in Christ with your current friends? Or is your Christianity a secret thing? They need what you have. Don't let the enemy trick you into not sharing it!

10. A Real Friend Forgives Others

You won't travel too far down the road of friendship before you get hurt and hurt others. When that happens, being a real friend means forgiving others.

We are to forgive as Christ has forgiven us (Ephesians 4:32). When Jesus forgave us, He agreed to take upon Himself the consequences of our sin. He will not use our past offenses against us. That's what Jesus is asking us to do. "He who covers over an offense promotes love, but whoever repeats the matter separates close friends" (Proverbs 17:9).

We've come to see that unforgiveness of others is the number-one problem among Christians. Satan loves it when Christians fight or harbor grudges that separate them from one another. Make the choice to forgive. You can find additional help in step three of the Steps to Freedom in chapter 13 of this book and in chapter 11 of the book *Stomping Out the Darkness.*

A Real Friend Draws Real Friends

In addition to being a good friend we also need good friends. You will naturally want friends who display the qualities we've talked about. These are the qualities that attracted me (Dave) to my wife Grace—not to mention her great humor, looks, and intelligence. You will find that as you develop these qualities people will be attracted to you and want to be your friend.

Ultimately you'll probably want to find a true friend who might become a lifelong friend and lover, an intimate companion and mate. "The Lord God said, 'It is not good for the man to be alone; I will make a helper suitable for him'" (Genesis 2:18). For this reason a man will leave his father and his mother and be united to his wife; and they will become one flesh" (Genesis 2:24). Remember, you'll end up marrying someone who is a friend first, so select your friends carefully.

Jesus Is Your Best Friend

Have you ever wished that a certain person in your life would be your friend? Perhaps you thought, *I am going to do whatever I can to make him my friend.* Only you were disappointed because he had his own agenda and didn't share your desire for friendship. But consider what you already have. We are talking about the God of the universe—the most significant other that you could possibly have in your life. And He chose you!

Jesus is the best friend you could ever have. Many may desert you during times of trouble, but Jesus invites you to draw near to Him. In John 15:12-17, He says you are no longer a servant doing only what is commanded, without understanding the purpose. Jesus takes His friends into His confidence. In John 15:15 He says, "Everything that I learned from my Father I have made known to you." He also said, "But when he, the Spirit of truth, comes, he will guide you into all truth. . . . All that belongs to the Father is mine. That is why I said the Spirit will take from what is mine and make it known to you" (John 16:13,15). Jesus discloses Himself to us. We know Him. He is the friend who sticks closer than a brother, the One who stays with us through all adversity.

Another proof that Jesus is your best friend is that He purposely sacrificed Himself for you. "This is how we know what love is: Jesus Christ laid down his life for us" (1 John 3:16). Many people express the sentiment, "Oh, I wish Jesus was my friend." That wish has already been granted. He is your friend because He chose to be your friend. He chose *you.*

How Can I Be a Friend to Christ?

You may say, "I know Jesus is my friend, but how can I be a friend to Jesus?" First of all, let's go back to what makes a friend. The most important thing you can do is to be real with God. Open yourself up to Him, and be totally honest. He loves you and always has your best interests at heart.

Forgiving Yourself

God has forgiven every child of God. "Therefore, there is now no condemnation for those who are in Christ Jesus" (Romans 8:1). It can only do you harm to condemn yourself. When we can't accept ourselves, we have difficulty loving and accepting others.

Forgiving yourself is simply agreeing with God and receiving His forgiveness. When one counselor suggested a certain woman forgive herself for having an abortion, she suddenly came under great spiritual attack. She had already asked God's forgiveness, but forgiving herself was obviously where Satan wanted to keep her in bondage. After she forgave herself, the harassment she had lived with for so long stopped. The day after her appointment, she approached the counselor again and said, "My mind has never been so quiet and peaceful."

A young lady wrote:

Dear Dave and Neil,

For five agonizing years I was overcome with feelings of self-hatred, leading to anorexia which eventually lead to bulimia and laxative abuse. I never thought I would conquer these obstacles. I refused help and was conformed to my way of life. Then my youth pastor gave me a copy of *The Bondage Breaker* (Youth Edition). I must admit, I read the first six chapters without much conviction. Finally, one night, something in my head snapped. I recognized, after so many years, that I really did want to get well. I completed the book and dedicated my life to Christ.

Now I have found a fulfillment and a contented heart through the love of Christ. Learning that I should live my life for the Lord, and not the world, has provided me with unimaginable joy.

Very Sincerely,
Jackie

Jackie found freedom. Just as Christ forgave her, she could forgive herself and experience the joy and happiness that is every Christian's birthright.

Because you're Christ's friend, you can love Him back by obeying Him. And by God's grace, He will enable you to bear fruit and to love others.

Now take some time to let the Lord reveal the truth about your current friendships. Are they from God or the enemy? Also let Him reveal to you the kind of friend He wants you to be.

- ❏ Sometimes it's more important to me that my friends like me rather than that I please God.
- ❏ I sometimes look to my friends to meet my need for security, significance, and acceptance.
- ❏ I feel like the enemy has targeted my friendships because I have very few people with whom I communicate deeply.
- ❏ I am often influenced by my friends to do things I know are wrong.
- ❏ I sometimes hang around certain people in order to be popular even though I know they are not really my friends.
- ❏ I have few friends I can really trust and who are truly loyal to me.
- ❏ I admit that I have closed the door to a true friendship because I thought it would make me unpopular with others.
- ❏ I admit that I have not encouraged my friends the way I should.
- ❏ I sometimes lie to my friends because I think it's what they want to hear.
- ❏ I sometimes refuse to forgive friends who have hurt me, even though I know God wants me to.

Lord I confess that I have not been the friend
You have called me to be by_____.
Thank You for forgiving me. I'm glad that I'm
always Your friend. In Jesus' name I pray. Amen.

Purity Pointers

Read: Review each of the Scriptures in the "Real Friend" list. Select one and memorize it.

Reflect: 1. How often do you talk with Jesus? What do you talk about most? Are you honest with Him? What keeps you from being honest?

2. Have you accepted Jesus' sacrifice and have you forgiven yourself?

3. What is a real friend to you? Who is your closest friend? Are you a real friend to that person?

Respond: Why not settle it once and for all? You are Christ's friend because He appointed and chose you personally. You can respond to Him right now with this prayer:

Lord, I thank You for Your friendship and I accept You as the best friend in my life because I can always be honest with You. I know that You love me and will never leave me. Lord, I want to be an unselfish friend to others like You are to me. Enable me to walk in the light and speak the truth in love with everyone I know. I confess that bad company corrupts good morals, and I renounce the lies of Satan that would damage my relationships. I pray that You would enable me to love others as You have loved me. In Jesus' precious name. Amen.

> *But seek first his kingdom, and his righteousness;*
> *and all these things shall be added to you.*
> *Matthew 6:33*

CHAPTER THREE

Dating in 3D

The important issue is not to find the right person, but to be the right person.

—Greg Laurie[1]

The way some teenagers go about it, you would think there was nothing to attract people of the opposite sex except sex.

—Tom Watson, Jr.[2]

The phone rings. Andrea yells, "I'll get it," and makes a mad dash for the phone. Her heart begins to pound with excitement as she realizes it's Monte, that cute guy she met at senior high camp last summer.

"Uhh . . . hi. Say," Monte's voice cracks. Clearing his throat, he starts over. "Yeah, I was wondering. Are you doing anything this Saturday?"

"Oh I don't know," she fires back. "Why? What did you have in mind?"

"Well, my parents aren't home. I thought we might get together and study biology. You know, that section on human anatomy, or we could go for a drive or something."

That conversation probably sounds familiar. Some would call it an invitation for a date. But look closely. It's really a set-up for temptation. The fear that you'll never be loved may cause you to become overanxious, to say yes before asking the right questions or finding out a person's true motives or establishing a friendship first. The way to stay out of trouble is to select your friends and dates prayerfully and to strategically plan you dates ahead of time.

The Dating Trap

Some people get caught in the "I just have to be dating" trap. When I (Dave) was in high school, and even in college, most of my friends thought they had to be dating. If you weren't dating, people treated you like you had some kind of disease. But the Lord doesn't want us to be obsessed about any other relationship except the relationship we have with Him. Jesus said, "So do not worry, saying, 'What shall we eat?' or 'What shall we drink?' or 'What shall we wear?' For the pagans run after all these things, and your Heavenly Father knows that you need them. But seek first His kingdom and His righteousness, and all these things will be given to you as well. Therefore do not worry about tomorrow, for tomorrow will worry about itself. Each day has enough trouble of its own" (Matthew 6:31-34).

Your Heavenly Father knows you need friendships

and desire a mate. But seek *first* your Father's plans for you and His kingdom, and all these things will be given to you when you are ready for them and need them. So don't spend time worrying about who you'll date tomorrow. Tomorrow will be filled with enough trouble. Why add to it?

Jesus reminds us to seek the Lord in two ways. First, we are to seek His Kingdom. What does it mean to seek the Lord's Kingdom? It means to put the Lord's plans ahead of your plans, to let Him call the shots and determine what goes on in your life, even who you date. In the ancient Hebrew culture people didn't date! In fact, men and women didn't even get to pick who they would marry. A man's father selected a bride for his son. None of us would want to go back to those days, but let's not miss the point. God, our Heavenly Father, wants to pick who we date and who we marry. We're seeking God's Kingdom when we let Him choose who we date. If you think about it, it's not that risky because God knows our needs and desires and wants to please us and give us what is really best for us. Psalm 37:4-7 says,

> Delight yourself in the LORD and he will give you the desires of your heart. Commit your way to the LORD; trust in him and he will do this: He will make your righteousness shine like the dawn, the justice of your cause like the noonday sun. Be still before the LORD and wait patiently for him; do not fret when men succeed in their ways, when they carry out their wicked schemes.

To delight yourself in the Lord means to look to God for your sense of security and significance and to fulfill your need for love and acceptance. The real question isn't who are you going to date, but who are you? Not what's your dating relationship like, but what's your relationship with Jesus like?

Secondly, God wants us to seek His righteousness. That means God wants us to live out our lives the same way Jesus lived out His. Jesus depended totally on His Father. ("Father . . . not my will, but yours be done," Luke 22:42.) Right now you might be thinking "Yeah, God probably won't let me date until I'm 30!" If that's really a concern, then ask for God's help. Philippians says "Do not be anxious about anything, but in everything, by prayer and petition, with thanksgiving, present your requests to God. And the peace of God, which transcends all understanding, will guard your hearts and your minds in Christ Jesus" (Philippians 4:6,7). But be patient. A little later in the same portion of Scripture Paul says, "I have learned to be content whatever the circumstances" (Philippians 4:11). Let your heart be satisfied with the knowledge that God has things under control. He hasn't forgotten you and He knows just what you want and need.

Don't get in a rush. Take time to get to know a person before you consider dating that person. Ask the right questions. Has he trusted in Christ? Is she right with God and currently walking in fellowship with Him? What's his motive? Why does she want to date? If you get the wrong answers say, "I'm sorry, but I know things wouldn't work out." Speak the truth in love. If you're asked why you won't date, be honest. Shoot straight. It may lead the other person to Christ or back to Him. Don't compromise—accept nothing less than God's best. First Corinthians 13:4-7 reminds us:

Love is patient, love is kind. It does not
envy, it does not boast, it is not proud. It is not
rude, it is not self-seeking, it is not easily
angered, it keeps no record of wrongs. Love
does not delight in evil but rejoices with the
truth. It always protects, always trusts,
always hopes, always perseveres.

Don't let the enemy steal your hope. God will provide the companionship and friendship you need.

Dangerous and Deadly Dating

One question you may be asking is, What is dating
anyway? Dating is difficult to define in our culture, but
you might consider a date as a preplanned meeting for
the specific purpose of evaluating a relationship; does it
have potential that goes beyond friendship? With that
definition in mind, should a Christian date a non-
Christian?

Well, nowhere in the Bible does it say, "Thou shalt
not date an unsaved person or your brain will melt."
God's Word does, however, say:

Do not be yoked together with unbelievers. For what do righteousness and wickedness have in common? Or what fellowship
can light have with darkness? What harmony
is there between Christ and Belial? What does
a believer have in common with an unbeliever? What agreement is there between the temple of God and idols? For we are the temple of
the living God. As God has said: "I will live
with them and walk among them, and I will

> be their God, and they will be my people.
> Therefore come out from them and be sepa-
> rate," says the Lord. "Touch no unclean thing,
> and I will receive you. I will be a Father to you,
> and you will be my sons and daughters," says
> the Lord Almighty (2 Corinthians 6:14-18).

God doesn't leave us in the dark when it comes to marriage. He makes it clear that we are not to marry an unbeliever, because spiritually we will have nothing in common with the other person. So, if you are not to marry an unbeliever, why would you want to date one? Why risk falling in love with someone you know you can't commit to? We have run into many people who fell in love with an unsaved person. Almost all of these people said they thought they could change the other person or lead him to Christ. Keep in mind that your future husband or wife will be someone whom you first date. This is a strong motivation not to date unbelievers. Also, God asks us to "Come out from them." That doesn't mean we never talk to unsaved people. We are called to witness to them (Acts 1:8). But we must be careful we are not negatively influenced by them.

Also, you need to wait until you are mature enough to handle dating. Consider these stats:

- 91% of girls who began to date at age 12 had sex before graduation.
- 56% of girls who began to date at age 13 had sex before graduation.
- 53% of girls who began to date at age 14 had sex before graduation.
- 40% of girls who began to date at age 15 had sex before graduation.

- 20% of girls who began to date at age 16 had sex before graduation.[3]

We hope you get the picture. Maturity does not just come with age; it's also determined by how well we follow and imitate Christ. How well people see Christ in us. Some people in their 30s are still not ready to date.

Diane Sawyer reported on "Prime Time Live" that 33 percent of American girls have had sexual intercourse by the end of the ninth grade and 70 percent by the end of high school. She interviewed several sexually active teenage girls, some as young as 13, who claimed to have had as many as ten different partners. At the end of the segment, Sawyer reported, "Every single one of these sexually active girls confided in us that they wish they'd said no."[4]

If you date too early, date non-Christians, or go often on unplanned dates, you are running red lights and moving into what can be called dangerous dating. If you run all three of these red lights, you've moved into deadly dating. The Bible offers us an example of someone who thought he could run a red light and not get hurt. His name was Samson.

Samson's Dating Life

Samson struggled with sexual sin, and it literally cost him his life. It isn't too hard for us to relate to his circumstances now that we live in the age of AIDS.

Samson was the strongest man to ever live. He makes Arnold Schwarzenegger look like a wimp. You may recall some of the familiar stories, but do you know what Scripture records as the first words out of Samson's own mouth? "I have seen a woman." We

don't have to spend too much time wondering what was on his mind. Apparently, Samson didn't know much about friendships with women because he told his parents, "I have seen a Philistine woman in Timnah; now get her for me as my wife" (Judges 14:2). How romantic! "His father and mother replied, 'Isn't there an acceptable woman among your relatives or among all our people? Must you go to the uncircumcised Philistines to get a wife?' But Samson said to his father, 'Get her for me. She's the right one for me'" (Judges 14:2,3).

God isn't against interracial marriages, but He is concerned about who we worship, who we call our god. As you might have guessed, Samson's marriage didn't last long.

You would think Samson would have learned his lesson and not made that mistake again, but he's a lot like us! The next woman he fell for was a Philistine named Delilah. He once again set himself up for heartache by getting entangled with a non-believer and falling in love. Delilah didn't have Samson's interests at heart. She wasn't looking for true love and companionship. She didn't want to make a marriage commitment. She just wanted to set him up, so that she would receive a reward from the Philistines.

Delilah worked her trap well, using all the right words: "Samson, how can you say, 'I love you,' when you won't confide in me? Tell me the secret of your great strength." (See Judges 16:15.) At first Samson wouldn't tell her. He made up little stories about what needed to be done to control him and render him helpless. None of them worked. But Delilah was persistent and continued to wear him down. Finally, he told her. "Then the Philistines seized him, gouged out his eyes and took him down to Gaza. Binding him with bronze shackles, they set him to grinding in the prison" (Judges 16:21).

Some will tell you they love you. Others will challenge your love for them. Remember—true love doesn't pressure someone's purity. Delilah affected Samson's life in a big way, and your life will be affected by those you date.

Treat Them Right

Dating is a serious responsibility. God expects you to treat the people you date the same way Jesus would treat them. Guys, respect each girl and treat her the way you would want another guy to treat your future wife. Proverbs 5:21 says, "For a man's ways are in full view of the LORD, and he examines all his paths."

The time will come when you fall in love and your husband-or wife-to-be will ask you, "Have you ever, you know, had sex with anyone else?" You will either be able to look that special person right in the eyes and say, "No, I waited for you," or your eyes will hit the floor.

If you set up the right dating standards, it's a lot

easier to maintain your purity. If you have poor dating habits, look out. You're headed for a fall!

Dating Boundaries

If you want to have a positive dating experience, determine the boundaries ahead of time, make sure your date is well planned, and have a specific destination. By the time I (Dave) entered college I had finally figured out that it was no fun to date unless I knew the other person well. I had survived too many of those horrible dates where you both stare at each other, not knowing what to say.

Dating boundaries are usually perceived as a negative. Who wants boundaries? We want freedom! Well, God doesn't give us boundaries to imprison us but to ensure our safety. He wants to guard us from evil and guide us to His perfect will.

Boundary #1: Date People You Know Well

My wife Grace and I were good friends for quite sometime before she looked at me one day and said, "Hey, are we, you know, dating?" "I guess we are," I said. One of the first boundaries you need to make for yourself is that you won't date anyone you don't know well. Blind dates or last-minute dates can be invitations to trouble. We've heard many horrible accounts of date rape. Don't date anyone you don't know well. It's just not safe.

Boundary #2: Go on a Planned Date

A planned date ensures that you won't accidentally find yourself parked in the woods, out of gas, in temptation's trap. Ask your date where you're going. If there isn't a plan, don't go. If the plan sounds like an invitation to trouble, then pass. You need to avoid tempting situations. Romans 13:14 reminds us to "put on the Lord Jesus Christ and make no provision for the flesh in regard to its lusts" (NASB). Only go to safe places where you're sure you won't be tempted sexually and you know you're protected from any possibility of date rape. Group dating with other believers is a good idea because it ensures your safety and testimony.

What we're really talking about here is accountability. Ecclesiastes 4:9,10 says, "Two are better than one, because they have a good return for their work: If one falls down, his friend can help him up. But pity the man who falls and has no one to help him up!"

Boundary #3: Date Strong Believers

You want to date someone who has God's interests at heart and not their hormones. Non-believers can only imitate a walk in the Spirit, but a true believer who is strong in the Lord can help you avoid sexual temptation. Galatians 5:16 tells us, "Walk by the Spirit and you will not carry out the desire of the flesh" (NASB). When you date a strong believer, sexual temptation doesn't stop. All of us can still be tempted, accused, and deceived, but when both of you are believers, you are more likely to spot the enemy's plans and submit yourselves to God for help. "Therefore encourage one another and build each other up, just as in fact you are doing" (1 Thessalonians 5:11).

Boundary #4: Pray and Read God's Word Together

"Pray! On a date? Are you crazy?"
Most couples probably don't pray when they go out

together, but they should. If you want more than a superficial relationship, if you really want to know this person intimately, pray together. Nothing lets you know a person's heart for God like prayer.

God promised that He would draw near to us when we draw near to Him (James 4:8). One purpose of dating is to get to know the other person, but it is also an opportunity to grow closer to God. In a healthy relationship, there is the freedom to discuss the Lord and His Word together. Jeremiah 15:16 says, "When your words came, I ate them; they were my joy and my heart's delight, for I bear your name, O LORD God Almighty." Of course, you want joy and delight in your dating life.

Boundary #5: Worship and Witness Together

Hebrews 12:2 tells us to "fix our eyes on Jesus, the author and perfecter of our faith, who for the joy set before him endured the cross, scorning its shame, and sat down at the right hand of the throne of God." Fixing our eyes on Jesus is easy at church or youth group gatherings, but what happens when you're away from your familiar Christian surroundings? Do people still see Christ in you? Every date should have a spiritual side to it because you're a spiritual being. God is always with you. He indwells you, so you should always have an attitude of worship. If the person you're dating is two-faced, acting one way at church but hell-on-wheels everywhere else, the best thing you can do for yourself is let go. The only thing you're really losing is a heartache.

Now You Tell Me!

Maybe you're presently involved in a dating relationship that you know is not from God. But your heart and feelings are telling you to hold on—this might be love. "Okay," you tell yourself, "I know he doesn't know Christ personally, but I'm sure it will work out." Or maybe you're afraid this is your one and only chance at love. But if you have to compromise God's Word or your purity, it's not love.

God is love, and He always wants the best for you. God is all powerful and He can bring the right people into your life. God is all knowing and He knows how to show you who that special person is. Remember—God created you for a love relationship with Himself. Nurture your relationship with God first, and all the other important relationships will fall into place.

The Right Attitude

It's important now that you take some time and ask God to reveal to you any of Satan's evil lies about dating. Pray out loud and ask God if you have the right attitude toward dating.

> Dear Lord, I ask You to show me if I have the right attitude toward dating. I want to keep my ways pure and follow Your Word (Psalm 119:11). I choose to fix my eyes on Jesus and His ways (Hebrews 12:2). I believe God's Word is the only reliable guide for how I should relate to others. I have trusted Jesus to save me, so I know I'm His child. I ask You to reveal to my mind any way that I have been deceived by the father of lies concerning my dating relationships. I ask You, Lord, to look deep inside me and reveal to me my true

attitudes and actions. In Jesus' name I pray. Amen.

If God brings one of the following areas to mind, check that item. If He brings to your mind an item that's not on the list, be sure and deal with that as well.

- ❑ I sometimes date just to increase my popularity or so people won't think there's something wrong with me.
- ❑ I sometimes date just to explore another person sexually.
- ❑ I sometimes wear suggestive clothing just to get attention.
- ❑ I sometimes give in to physical temptation just to hold the relationship together.
- ❑ I sometimes date people I believe will boost my self-worth.
- ❑ I am only content or happy when I'm dating.
- ❑ I will date people regardless of their faith.
- ❑ I sometimes go against my parents and date people they don't approve of.
- ❑ I sometimes date people I know God doesn't want me to date.
- ❑ I'm afraid that God will forget me and my need for love and companionship.

If any of the above statements are true for you, use the following prayer for the purpose of confession. Pray each item separately and out loud.

Lord, I confess that I have disobeyed You by _____. Thank You for Your forgiveness. I choose to turn my back on my old

ways and follow You according to Your Word.
In Jesus' name I pray. Amen.

Purity Pointers

Read: Look up the following verses. Remember—
God isn't against any particular race. He is
concerned about how and what we worship.
Describe how God feels about our relationships.

Deuteronomy 7:3,4

1 Corinthians 7:38

Exodus 34:16

Ezra 9:1,2

Ezra 9:12

Reflect: 1. What is a planned date? Why is a planned
date so important?

2. How can dating when you're too young
lead to trouble? How old do you think you
should be before you should date? Have you
talked to Mom and Dad about it?

3. Do any of the dating boundaries listed in
this chapter seem unreasonable to you?
What are some of the boundaries you want
in your dating life?

4. Do you think a Christian should date a non-Christian? What are some of the regrets you might have later if you date a non-Christian?

Respond: Dear Heavenly Father, more than anything else I want my relationship with You to have first place in my life. I know I can trust You to meet my needs for love and acceptance. So I give my dating life to You. I ask for Your wisdom and guidance concerning my relationship with the opposite sex. Help me to be patient and not compromise. I want Your best for me. Thank You for Your Word and how it gives me the direction I need. In Jesus' name I pray. Amen.

CHAPTER FOUR

Am I Really in Love?

Today it is very common to hear someone talk about "falling in love" with another person. But have you ever stopped to ask yourself what these words actually mean? What changes take place in the minds of men and women who have fallen in love? How can they know when love is genuine? Can they be fooled, thinking they are "in love" when they aren't? What is necessary to keep their love alive?

Can you answer these questions about the meaning of love? Most young people cannot.

—Dr. James Dobson[1]

Perhaps no word in the English language is so commonly used as is the word *love*. It pops up everywhere in our conversations: "I love my car," "I love my dog," "I love my wife." But I obviously don't care for all these things in the same way. So what is the true meaning of this word? The dictionary defines *love* as "a strong affection," but that doesn't tell us a lot. Perhaps the best way to understand the meaning of true love is to let God define it. We want our meaning of love to match up with His Word.

The Meaning of Love

The words *love, loved,* and *loves* appear over 700 times in the Bible. We could check out all the ways God uses love in the Bible and come up with our definition for true love, but that would take quite some time. So how about if we check out just seven key verses, remembering that God has many more ways for us to learn about love?

- Romans 5:8: "But God demonstrates his own love for us in this: While we were still sinners, Christ died for us."

God is love, therefore true love is unconditional.

- Jeremiah 31:3: "The LORD appeared to us in the past, saying: "I have loved you with an everlasting love; I have drawn you with loving-kindness."

God's love is everlasting, therefore true love is commitment.

- Ephesians 2:4: "But because of his great love for us, God, who is rich in mercy . . ."

God's love is great, therefore true love is of the highest character.

- Galatians 2:20: "I have been crucified with Christ and I no longer live, but Christ lives in me. The life I live in the body, I live by faith in the Son of God, who loved me and gave himself for me."

God's love is giving, therefore true love is sacrificial.

- John 14:21: "Whoever has my commands and obeys them, he is the one who loves me. He who loves me will be loved by my Father, and I too will love him and show myself to him."

God's love is personal, therefore true love creates closeness.

- Romans 8:35: "Who shall separate us from the love of Christ? Shall trouble or hardship or persecution or famine or nakedness or danger or sword?"

God's love is unbreakable, therefore true love lasts.

- 1 John 3:16: "This is how we know what love is. Jesus Christ laid down his life for us. And we ought to lay down our lives for our brothers."

God's love meets my needs, therefore I'm able to meet the needs of others.

Four Kinds of Love

God shows us in His Word the ingredients for true

love. As you read the above verses, did you see that true love was far more than a feeling or warm emotion? Words like *sacrifice* and *commitment* must be in our definition as well.

You have probably heard some of your friends say, "I think I'm falling in love!" Maybe you have used that expression yourself. I (Dave) remember dating in college and hearing my dates tell me they loved me. It always felt good to hear those words, but I also realized that those who were saying them really didn't know me that well. I decided that I would refrain from speaking those words until I met my wife, wherever she was.

When I was a junior in college I met a girl named Grace, and we became friends. After a few months, we began to date. I explained right away that she would never hear me say I loved her because I was saving those words for my wife. I didn't know it at the time but that meant a lot to Grace because she too had many friends who had used those words recklessly with her. Finally, that special night arrived. I knew Grace was the woman God had handpicked for me.

I was very quiet that evening, something out of character for me. So Grace asked me, "What are you thinking about?" I sat quietly for a moment, then I said, "I'm thinking about how much I love you." Grace's eyes grew wide and she stared at me hard because she knew what the next words would be. "Will you marry me?" I asked. Without hesitating Grace fired back a "Yes!" "Did I just ask you to marry me?" I joked. "Yes," she answered with a look that said, "You better not try to take it back, buddy." But I had no intention of taking those words back, and I never will because true love is commitment.

I was attracted to Grace the first time I met her, but

being attracted to someone doesn't mean you love that person. Sometimes it's just infatuation. Someone has said that infatuation is just one set of glands calling out to another. You enjoy that feeling of excitement when you meet someone you're attracted to, but at this point you're not really looking at this person as someone you would like to marry. You may want to start a friendship, and when the friendship is solid, you may want to consider dating that person. This phase is sometimes called "puppy love." We are attracted to people and things because they make us feel good or turn us on. These desires are based on things we want. The Greeks called this kind of desire *epithumia*. It could mean a strong desire to do good or wrong. If you pursue desires that are wrong, you will compromise your purity.

A common word in the Bible for love is *phileo*, which means brotherly love, the kind you feel in friendships. This responsive love is given in return for something received. *Agape* love, on the other hand, gives no matter what it receives. Jesus demonstrated this kind of love when He died on the cross for us.

The Greek word *eros*, from which we get the word *erotic*, is never used in the Bible. It describes your body's craving for food and sex. These are natural desires that become sinful when you lose self-control and begin to ignore the needs of others.

There will come a time in your life when your dating will center around just one person. At that time you should be more mature in terms of your age and life experience. God has led you to someone you're compatible with. You share the same convictions about Jesus, your faith, and your purpose in life. You have seen puppy love come and go, and you sense you're ready for a deeper relationship. Still, how do you know

Attraction love (*epithumia*)	(Receives) An infatuation for people and things
Physical love (*eros*)	(Takes) Physical craving for food, comfort, and sex
Brotherly love (*phileo*)	(Gives and Takes) The reciprocal love between friends who care
Godly love (*agape*)	(Gives) Unconditionally meets the needs of others

Figure 4A—Four Kinds of Love

if your feelings are real love?

Earlier we talked about how we received a new life and identity in Christ, and now we are accepted, secure, and significant. I (Neil) wrote a book called *Living Free In Christ* that shows how Christ meets these important needs (see Figure 4B). The apostle John says, "We love, because He first loved us" (1 John 4:19). If *agape* love is meeting the needs of others, let's test ourselves to see if we really do love that other person.

The Acceptance Tests

1. The Belonging Test

First, realize that you belong to God (1 Corinthians 3:23; 6:19,20). Being made a part of the family of God meets an incredible need in our life to be accepted. Never compromise your purity to gain the acceptance of others because you will lose your true sense of belonging to God. Peer pressure is powerful because it

In Christ [2]

I AM ACCEPTED:

John 1:12	I am God's child.
John 15:15	I am Christ's friend.
Romans 5:1	I have been justified.
1 Cor. 6:17	I am united with the Lord, and I am one spirit with Him.
1 Cor. 6:19,20	I have been bought with a price. I belong to God.
1 Cor. 12:27	I am a member of Christ's body.
Ephesians 1:1	I am a saint.
Ephesians 1:5	I have been adopted as God's child.
Ephesians 2:18	I have direct access to God through the Holy Spirit.
Colossians 1:14	I have been redeemed and forgiven of all my sins.
Colossians 2:10	I am complete in Christ.

I AM SECURE:

Romans 8: 1,2	I am free from condemnation.
Romans 8:28	I am assured that all things work together for good.
Romans 8:31f	I am free from any condemning charge against me.
Romans 8:35f	I cannot be separated from the love of God.
2 Cor. 1:21,22	I have been established, anointed, and sealed by God.
Colossians 3:3	I am hidden with Christ in God.
Philippians 1:6	I am confident that the good work that God has begun in me will be perfected.
Philippians 3:20	I am a citizen of heaven.
2 Timothy 1:7	I have not been given a spirit of fear but of power, love, and a sound mind.
Hebrews 4:16	I can find grace and mercy in time of need.
1 John 5:18	I am born of God, and evil one cannot touch me.

I AM SIGNIFICANT:

Matt. 5:13,14	I am the salt and light of the earth.
John 15:1,5	I am a branch of the true vine, a channel of His life.
John 15:16	I have been chosen and appointed to bear fruit.
Acts 1:8	I am a personal witness of Christ's.
1 Cor. 3:16	I am God's temple.
2 Cor. 5:17f	I am a minister of reconciliation for God.
2 Cor. 6:1	I am God's coworker (1 Cor. 3:9).
Ephesians 2:6	I am seated with Christ in the heavenly realm.
Ephesians 2:10	I am God's workmanship.
Ephesians 3:12	I may approach God with freedom and confidence.
Philippians 4:13	I can do all things through Christ who strengthens me.

Figure 4B

ACCEPTANCE TESTS	SECURITY TESTS	SIGNIFICANCE TESTS
1. Belonging Test	1. Peace Test	1. Responsibilities Test
2. Unity Test	2. Separation	2. Intimacy Test
3. Respect Test	3. Time Test	3. Desires Test

Figure 4C —True Love Tests

appeals to our need to belong. Listen to these compromising thoughts:

"I know I can change him."

"He says he believes in God."

"She only acts that way to impress her friends. She'll grow out of it in time!"

If there's something you can't accept about the person you're dating right now, at this moment, then don't move ahead with the relationship. We have heard countless accounts of people who thought they could change their partner only to get stuck in a relationship where one person takes and doesn't know how to give. If a person does not know Christ, that person cannot meet your need to belong.

2. The Unity Test

Is there unity in your relationship? Do you believe the same things? Are you compatible? It's not that you have to like everything the other person likes, but you should have the same biblical beliefs about life. Do you enjoy praying together? Studying God's Word together? Witnessing together? These are all signs of unity with God and with each other.

3. The Respect Test

A college student who was dating a lovely Christian woman shared a profound thought: "I treat my girlfriend the way I think her future husband would want her to be treated." That couple is now happily married. Are you treated with respect? Do you treat your date with respect? If you're being pressured sexually then you're not being respected. True love is willing to wait for a complete commitment, a ring, and a wedding.

Let these tests help you determine if you're experiencing real love.

The Security Tests

1. The Peace Test

Colossians 3:15 says, "Let the peace of Christ rule in your hearts, since as members of one body you were called to peace. And be thankful." Do you have peace about the relationship? Do you sense a unity and oneness forming with the other person? A harmony? If not, end it immediately. Yes it will hurt, but it will hurt a lot worse if you let it go on. Take some time to be quiet and still before the Lord and ask Him if this relationship is from Him. He will answer.

2. The Separation Test

We travel a great deal with our conference schedules

and that means being separated from our wives and families. You should see our phone bills! The old expression, "absence makes the heart grow fonder," is really true. We miss our wives and children. They come to our minds constantly. So, if you find when you're separated from your steady date that you don't even think about that person, guess what? There isn't much there.

Have you ever gone camping and built a fire? If the wind can blow out your fire, it's because you didn't have much of a flame. But if the wind hits the fire and it burns even stronger, you've got a great flame. Love is like that.

3. The Time Test

True love means knowing the other person well, and there is just no substitute for time. Have you spent time with your loved one's family and has your loved one spent time with yours? Watch the other person when engaged in a competitive sport. How does he handle his emotions? How does she talk to the other players? Guys, how does your girl talk to her dad? Listen closely because that's how she will talk to you someday. Ladies, how does your guy talk to his mother? Is he rude and snippy? That's how he will talk to you. All these things take time to discover. All of us can put on a mask and pretend to be something we're not, but not over the long haul. True love will pass the test of time.

The Significance Tests

1. The Responsibilities Test

A lot of people today don't want any responsibilities. But when it comes to relationships you need to fulfill your end of the deal. We have a duty to perform. The Bible reminds husbands to love (*agape*) their wives, "just as Christ loved the church and gave himself up for her" (Ephesians 5:25). *Agape* love is the kind of self-sacrificing love that doesn't expect anything in return. This same passage goes on to say, "husbands ought to love [*agape*] their wives as their own bodies. He who loves [*agapes*] his wife loves himself" (Ephesians 5:28). One way to measure your feelings of love is to ask yourself if you can truly love this person with an *agape* type love. The Bible also tells women to love their husbands. Titus 2:4 says, "Then they can train the younger women to love [*phileo*] their husbands and children." But in this verse, the word *love* doesn't mean *agape*, it means *phileo*. Women are called to respond to their husband's love.

Also, we have a responsibility to care for our families. First Timothy 5:8 gives us this harsh warning: "If anyone does not provide for his relatives, and especially for his immediate family, he has denied the faith and is worse than an unbeliever." If you aren't ready to handle responsibility, then your love may need more time to develop.

2. The Intimacy Test

True love involves more than just familiarity in a relationship. True love means you know one another's convictions, not just what the beliefs are, but where the beliefs come from. You experience common understanding and know how to affirm each other and build each other up. You understand each other's strengths and weaknesses and you don't have any secrets from each other. "Therefore each of you must put off falsehood and speak truthfully to his neighbor, for we are all members of one body" (Ephesians 4:25).

3. The Desires Test

Since your significance is found in Christ, you need to "Delight yourself in the Lord and He will give you the desires of your heart" (Psalm 37:4). One way true love reveals itself in a relationship is through the discovery of similar desires. Many men and women get married only to find out that their spouse doesn't want anything to do with their life plans. We know of one pastor's wife who has nothing to do with her husband's ministry at the church, and another man who had to leave the mission field because his wife didn't like it and didn't sense a call to that ministry. Do you share the same desires in life (ministry, jobs, children, where you want to live, etc.) with the person you're beginning to love?

False, Fake, and Phony Love

Love is a serious thing and your heart is not a play-toy. Relationships that are mishandled, hurt. Don't play around with love or lead others on when you have no intention of developing a real relationship. Don't use your dating life to entertain yourself. Some seek love for the sake of adventure. If it's adventure you want, go to Disneyland and hit the Indiana Jones ride. If you just want to be loved or needed—hey, in Christ you are both loved and needed. Don't get your dating life and your identity confused. In Christ, you're already significant, secure, and you belong!

When I (Dave) traveled with Josh McDowell I would hear him say, "You have two fears—one, that you will never be loved, and secondly, that you'll never be able to love." Those fears come from the enemy. They are not from God because God has not given us a spirit of fear. Romans 8:15 says, "For you did not receive a spir-it that makes you a slave again to fear, but you received the Spirit of sonship. And by Him we cry, 'Abba, Father.'" Don't stay in a relationship because you think it might be your only shot at love. And if you have to com-promise your purity or your faith, then it's not love and it's not worth it. Remember—God is in control.

Love Versus Lust

First Corinthians 13 is called the love chapter, and it will help you spot genuine love in a world that's full of the counterfeit. Take the time to read through this pow-erful chapter.

> If I speak in the tongues of men and of angels, but have not love, I am only a resounding gong or a clanging cymbal. If I have the gift of prophecy and can fathom all mysteries and all knowledge, and if I have a faith that can move mountains, but have not love, I am nothing. If I give all I possess to the poor and surrender my body to the flames, but have not love, I gain nothing. Love is patient, love is kind. It does not envy, it does not boast, it is not proud. It is not rude, it is not self-seeking, it is not easily angered, it keeps no record of wrongs. Love does not delight in evil but rejoices with the truth. It always protects, always trusts, always hopes, always perseveres. Love never fails. But where there are prophecies, they will cease; where there are tongues, they will be stilled; where there is knowledge, it will pass away. For we know in part and we prophesy in part, but when perfec-

tion comes, the imperfect disappears. When I was a child, I talked like a child, I thought like a child, I reasoned like a child. When I became a man, I put childish ways behind me. Now we see but a poor reflection as in a mirror; then we shall see face to face. Now I know in part; then I shall know fully, even as I am fully known. And now these three remain: faith, hope and love. But the greatest of these is love.

Love

1. Love is patient.

2. Love is kind.

3. Love does not envy.

4. Love does not boast.

5. Love is not proud.
6. Love is not rude.
7. Love is not self-seeking.
8. Love is not easily angered.
9. Love forgives others.

10. Love hates evil.

11. Love rejoices in the truth.

12. Love always protects.

13. Love always trusts.

Lust

1. Lust can't wait; it's impulsive.

2. Lust is critical; it wants its own way.

3. Lust seeks more than it earns.

4. Lust builds up self no matter who it hurts.

5. Lust is easily threatened.
6. Lust is disrespectful.
7. Lust is demanding.
8. Lust is moody and lashes out.
9. Lust says vengeance is mine.

10. Lust does anything to get its own way; it rationalizes.

11. Lust encourages lies and tries to hide sins.

12. Lust doesn't care who it hurts; it wants its own way.

13. Lust is jealous and suspicious.

14. Love always hopes.

14. Lust says, you blow it you're out.

15. Love always perseveres.

15. Lust backs out when times are tough.

16. Love never fails.

16. Lust stops when self isn't served.

17. Love is unending.

17. Lust lasts just a moment then flickers away.

18. Love is enduring.

18. Lust is insecure.

19. Love is faithful.

19. Lust will cheat on you.

20. Love is commitment.

20. Lust is not trustworthy.[3]

Ready for Marriage?

How can you know if you are ready for marriage? You may be saying, "Wait a minute. I know I'm not ready for marriage." That may be true now. But at some point you will meet that special person. And then the following tips may come in handy.

1. You're Ready When You Can Love Properly

You will know you're ready for marriage when you can love with a self-sacrificing type of love and respond to love the way you should. If you have accepted Christ you have the capacity to love because Christ is in you. God created marriage to be an earthly picture of our relationship with Him. How I love my wife shows me how I really love my God. If I'm not kind to a wife whom I can see, hear, and hold, how will I ever learn to love God whom I can't see, hold, and hear audibly? Don't say "I do" or "Will you?" until you are committed to love the way Jesus loves.

2. You're Ready When You Can Make a Total Commitment

If we could only pick one word to describe love, we would pick *commitment*. One reason so many marriages fail today is because they have no long-lasting commitment. A prevailing attitude is, "If it doesn't work out, I'll just get a divorce." But this isn't a bad car you're replacing here. What about God's desires, His plan for your life? The Bible says God hates divorce (Malachi 2:16).

So why even get married? Because with marriage, there is commitment—vows and promises before a group of people who are witnessing your marriage. Also, God condemns sex outside of marriage (1 Corinthians 6:9). You're ready for marriage when you can make a lifetime commitment to the person you love.

3. You're Ready When You Can Handle the Responsibility

Guys, are you ready to be a spiritual leader? To be the head of the home is an awesome spiritual responsibility. Are you trying to control each other, or are you developing self-control? If you're saying, "Hold on. I don't even have my own spiritual act together," then get your love life right with God first and then concentrate on your other relationships. Being a husband or a wife is a big deal. You will have financial responsibilities. Do you know where the money will come from to support a family? If not, you may not be ready for marriage.

4. You're Ready When You Both Have Common Desires

What are your desires for your marriage, family, and life? Do you and your loved one agree about the direction and path God has called you to follow? Or is it like a big fog came and took up residency in your head? If so, then wait until it lifts. You will never be sorry.

5. You're Ready When You Sense God's Perfect Peace

I (Dave) heard once about a baseball umpire who was a little late on making the call. The pitcher threw the ball to the catcher. Both the batter and the catcher turned to the ump to hear the call, but he just stood there silently. "What is it?" asked the catcher. "It ain't nothin until I call it," replied the umpire. Let peace be the umpire of your heart (Colossians 3:15). If deep in your heart you don't sense peace, wait.

If even one of the above areas isn't in place, you may not be ready for marriage. Don't worry though. God has it all planned out.

Purity Pointers

Read: Read through the seven key verses at the beginning of this chapter that we used to help define love: Romans 5:8; Jeremiah 31:3; Ephesians 2:4; Galatians 2:20; John 14:21; Romans 8:35; 1 John 3:16.

Reflect: 1. How would you define true love? List the key words you would use in your definition. How is the world's definition of love different from God's?

2. First Corinthians 13 tells us what true love is like. What areas in your life did

you sense God telling you needed improvement?

3. How can you know if you're really ready for marriage?

Respond: Dear Heavenly Father, thank You for Your great love for me. I know that I have not been completely loving toward others. Please forgive me for my selfishness. I choose now to follow Your example and love my neighbor as myself. I ask You to give me wisdom so that I might understand my feelings. Show me what real love is. In Jesus' name I pray. Amen.

God's Design and Purity

CHAPTER FIVE

God's View on Sex

God and sex are connected. God *created* sex. For a man and a woman in the bond of marriage, sex is designed as a good and powerful gift. It allows them to share with each other the essence of who they are—physically, emotionally and spiritually. In an environment of love and commitment, there can be no more powerful expression of exclusive intimacy than sex.

—Bill Hybels[1]

You may have heard that the way to learn how to recognize counterfeit money is not to study counterfeit money. You study the real thing—genuine currency—so thoroughly that you will quickly spot a phony bill if you look at it closely. This should be our approach when contrasting Satan's perversion of sex with God's perfect plan.

It's the truth that sets us free, not a knowledge of error (John 8:32). It is vital that we understand God's design for sex and marriage.

God created us as sexual beings—male and female. Gender is determined at conception, and the entire sexual anatomy is present at birth. Even the molecular structure of a skin sample, when studied under a microscope, will reveal an infant's sexual identity. God is not anti-sex; He created sex! David proclaimed, "You created my inmost being; you knit me together in my mother's womb. I praise you because I am fearfully and wonderfully made; your works are wonderful" (Psalm 139:13,14).

Wrong Perceptions

Viewing sex as evil is not the way to respond to what God created and pronounced good. "For everything God created is good, and nothing is to be rejected if it is received with thanksgiving, because it is consecrated by the Word of God and prayer" (1 Timothy 4:4,5). Sex is not wrong or dirty in itself. But Satan is evil and is able to distort what God created. Denying our sexuality and being afraid to talk about our sexual development is playing into the devil's hand.

A Plan for All Time

God's ideal plan for marriage was outlined in the Garden of Eden before Adam and Eve sinned: "A man will leave his father and mother and be united to his wife, and they will become one flesh" (Genesis 2:24). To be united means to be glued together. An incredible bond is formed when two people become one flesh. It is one man and one woman forming an inseparable union that is meant to last a lifetime.

God commanded Adam and Eve to make babies and fill the earth with their offspring. Sounds like a fun command! But there was some responsibility involved. And so, when Adam and Eve sinned in the garden, they marred God's beautiful plan. But let's not be too hard on them. Had any of us been in the garden, we probably would have done the same thing.

God did not walk out on Adam and Eve though. He stuck to His plan for man, woman, and their sexual relationship, despite the fall. He even used human marriage and proper sex as the vehicle for redeeming fallen humanity. God made a promise to Abraham: "Through your offspring all nations on earth will be blessed, because you have obeyed me" (Genesis 22:18). The offspring God was talking about was Jesus Christ (Galatians 3:16), who would bless the whole world by providing salvation through His death and resurrection. And there was another part to God's plan for marriage after the fall. Ever since Adam and Eve, the vows and promises between a husband and wife have been a picture of the covenant relationship between God and His people. The church is called the bride of Christ (Revelation 19:7), and He desires to receive to Himself a bride who is holy and blameless, "without stain or wrinkle or any other blemish" (Ephesians 5:26,27). The purity and faithfulness of a Christian marriage should be a picture of the purity and faithfulness God desires in our relationship with Him.

God Doesn't Condemn Sex

God doesn't condemn sex—He condemns the *misuse*

of sex. God made sex to be enjoyed. If you doubt that, read the Song of Solomon. But the Bible condemns sexual immorality for two important reasons.

First, unfaithfulness or sexual sin violates God's plan for purity in human marriage. Check out Hebrews 13:4. God says, "Marriage should be honored by all, and the marriage bed kept pure, for God will judge the adulterer and all the sexually immoral." When you become sexually involved with someone other than your spouse, whether physically or mentally through lust and fantasy, you shatter God's design. You bond with that person, staining the "one man and one woman" picture (1 Corinthians 6:16,17). We were created to become one flesh with only one other person.

Second, when you commit a sexual sin you deface the picture of God's covenant relationship with His people which your future marriage was designed to portray.

Think about it: A loving, pure, committed relationship between a husband and wife is God's illustration to the world of the loving, pure, committed relationship He desires with His body, the church. Every act of sexual sin among His people tarnishes that illustration. That's why God condemns the misuse of sex. He's not some big cosmic ogre in the sky who says, "That looks fun, so I think I'll call that sin and make lots of rules that say no one is allowed to do that!" Something is wrong or sinful because it doesn't line up with God's character. It's something Jesus would never do. On the other hand, something is right or holy because it lines up with God's character. It's something Jesus would do.

The Old Testament Plan

Abraham's descendants found themselves in slavery to Egypt. And so, God raised up Moses to deliver His people and provide for them a law to govern their relationships in the Promised Land, including their sexual ones. Six of the Ten Commandments listed in Exodus 20 deal with marital fidelity.

You shall have no other gods before me (verse 3). Sex outside of marriage violates this commandment because it elevates sexual pleasure above our relationship with God. We serve a jealous God. He won't tolerate a rival, including the god of our impure appetites.

Honor your father and your mother (verse 12). Sin of any kind, including sexual sin, brings shame and dishonor to our parents.

You shall not commit adultery (verse 14). God ordained sex to be confined to marriage. Adultery—sex outside of marriage—is a sin against your marriage partner and God (Genesis 39:9).

You shall not steal (verse 15). The adulterer robs his spouse of the intimacy of their relationship and steals from his illicit partner sexual pleasure that doesn't belong to him.

You shall not give false testimony (verse 16). Marriage is a covenant made before God and human witnesses. Sexual sin breaks the marriage vow. In effect, the unfaithful partner lies about being faithful to his or her spouse. The adulterer often continues lying to cover up the sin.

You shall not covet (verse 17). To covet is to desire something that doesn't belong to you. All sexual sin begins with a desire for someone or some experience that is not rightfully yours. The commandments of God are not to punish us or restrict our fun but rather to protect us and to provide for a great marriage.

The Old Testament also assures us that God designed sex within the confines of marriage for pleasure as well as making babies. The Song of Solomon portrays the joys of physical love in courtship and marriage. Furthermore, the law directed that the first year of marriage should be reserved for marital adjustment and enjoyment: "When a man takes a new wife, he shall not go out with the army, nor be charged with any duty; he shall be free at home one year and shall give happiness to his wife whom he has taken" (Deuteronomy 24:5 NASB).

As God's plan of redemption unfolded in the Old Testament, Satan was always there attempting to ruin it. On the eve of Christ's birth the Jews were in political bondage to Rome and in spiritual bondage to their bad leaders. The glory of God had departed from Israel. Satan had apparently foiled God's plan. But even though Israel's moral and spiritual fabric was shredded, God miraculously preserved her and used her to provide the world's Redeemer. Abraham's seed—Jesus Christ—would one day make His entrance (John 1:14). The blessing of Abraham would be extended to all the nations of the world in Christ.

The New Testament Plan

What was God's plan for Christian marriage after the cross in a world still dark with sin? The answer is found in 1 Thessalonians 4:3-5: "This is the will of God, your sanctification; that is, that you abstain from sexual immorality; that each of you know how to possess his own vessel in sanctification and honor, not in lustful passion, like the Gentiles who do not know God" (NASB).

The word *possess* means to take for yourself. The word *vessel* can mean "wife" (see 1 Peter 3:7) or "body." Bible scholars have varying opinions on which one it is; take it both ways and you won't go wrong. So verse 4 of 1 Thessalonians can be translated, "That each of you know how to take a wife for himself in sanctification and honor," or "That each one of you know how to control your own body in sanctification and honor." The word *abstain* is rarely used in the Bible, but when it is it means just one thing: don't do it, go away from, depart or distance yourself. God's plan is the same in the New Testament as it was in the Old Testament: a one-man one-woman marriage under God which is free of sexual immorality. By following God's plan we sow seeds of righteousness in His kingdom for ourselves and for future generations.

We can apply the instruction in 1 Thessalonians 4 to several specific areas of sexual temptation.

God's Views on Premarital Sex

It is common in our culture for couples who think they are in love to sleep together and even live together before marriage or if they think they may get married. We hear justifications such as, "Love is what counts; who needs a marriage certificate?" or "How can we know if we're sexually compatible unless we sleep together?" Our world places a high value on physical attraction and sexual compatibility in finding a partner. But engaging in premarital sex is not the way God wants us to seek a life partner.

Outward appearance and sexual appeal may be part of what attracts you to another person, but neither has the power to hold a couple together. Physical attraction is like perfume. You smell the fragrance when you put it on, but within minutes your sense of smell is saturated and you barely notice the scent. Similarly, unless you go beyond physical attraction to know the real person, the relationship won't last.

Dating is not like shopping for a good-looking, comfortable pair of shoes; it is the process of finding God's will for a lifetime marriage partner. Commitment to Christ and beauty of character far outweigh physical attraction and sex appeal in importance. Read 1 Corinthians 6.

God's Views on Extramarital Sex

Doug and Katy came to see me (Neil) years ago because they were having marital problems. In an angry moment Doug had told his wife that she didn't satisfy him sexually as had a previous girlfriend. In tears Katy told me how hard she tried to be like that other girl, something which was impossible for her!

Marital unfaithfulness is rooted in comparison. Originally you are attracted to your potential mate's appearance, personality, and other qualities. Of all the people you know, this person seems made just for you, and you seem made for him or her. So you commit yourselves to each other "till death do us part."

Once you are married, all comparisons must end. You may meet someone who looks better to you, more like a movie star. One who seems more sensitive and caring, or who shows deeper spiritual zeal. It doesn't matter. You're with the person God gave you. The best-possible-mate contest is over, and you and your spouse both won! As a Christian, your first commitment is to Christ, the most important relationship you have. Your marriage is a picture of that union, and no other relationship must be allowed to deface that picture. The pathway to marital happiness and fulfillment is found in pouring yourself into loving, serving, and fulfilling that person.

Many people who end up in extramarital affairs say that they were bored with the sex they got at home. They're not bored with their partners; they're bored with sex because they have depersonalized it. When the focus is on the sex act, the partner as a sex object, and personal sexual satisfaction, boredom is likely. But when the focus is on nurturing the relationship and fulfilling the dreams and expectations of your mate, married life—including sex—remains an exciting and rewarding experience.

God's Views on Fantasy

There it was again, the thought to pull off the freeway and rent a sexually explicit video. Even though

Scott was in high school, the guy at the video store never asked any questions. Scott had prayed repeatedly against the impulse, but as he sped closer to the off ramp a conflict raged within him. He knew his actions would displease God. He knew he would feel ashamed when it was all over. He knew he would be embarrassed if his mom or dad came home unexpectedly and found him acting out his fantasy. But he was propelled to the video store like a heroin addict to a fix.

Once he took the off ramp Scott was hooked again. But after watching the movie that afternoon, he was again flooded with shame and guilt. "Lord, what am I going to do?" he cried. He had told no one about his ongoing struggle and repeated failure in this area. He felt weak and alone. Even God seemed distant and unavailable.

So Scott did what he always did: He hid his feelings and guilt deep inside and went on with the charade of the pure, outgoing, happy Christian guy. Eventually his despair would lessen and he could relax until the old urges returned and pulled him under again.

Sexual fantasy may be regarded by many as harmless self-pleasuring. But God wants us to abstain from it for at least three different reasons.

First, under Jesus' guideline for adultery in Matthew 5:27,28, sexual immorality in the mind carries the same weight as sexual immorality in the flesh: "You have heard that it was said, 'Do not commit adultery.' But I tell you that anyone who looks at a woman lustfully has already committed adultery with her in his heart." You may be able to avoid the personal embarrassment, public scandal, or potential diseases of a physical affair. But in God's eyes, an affair in the mind is the same as the real thing. It is a violation of moral purity.

Second, according to James 1:14,15, sexual immorality

in the mind can lead to a sexually immoral act: "Each one is tempted when, by his own evil desire, he is dragged away and enticed. Then, after desire has conceived, it gives birth to sin; and sin, when it is full-grown, gives birth to death." You may think your secret is safe inside you, but "out of the overflow of the heart the mouth speaks" (Matthew 12:34). What is sown and nurtured as a seed in the heart will eventually flower as a deed.

Third, sexual fantasy depersonalizes sex and devalues people. For the person caught up in sexual fantasy, sex is not a facet of mutual joy and sharing in the marital relationship but an avenue for personal pleasure. Sex objects are not regarded as persons created in God's image, much less someone's daughter or son. Treating others as objects for personal gratification goes against everything the Bible teaches about the dignity and value of human life.

Remember, God sets up these boundaries in order to give you the best possible sex life *in* marriage. He loves you!

What About the "M" Word?

The Bible is silent on the topic of the "M" word, masturbation, and Christians are widely divided in their opinions about it. We certainly don't want to add any restrictions that God doesn't intend, nor do we want to contribute to the judgment already being heaped on people. But we've met so many Christians who feel guilty after masturbating. If you masturbate, or have been thinking about trying it, ask yourself the following questions:

1. Do you use masturbation as the physical release for your sexual fantasies? If you masturbate as you fantasize

about having sex with models in a magazine, characters in a novel or on the screen, or real or imagined persons in your mind, you are only underscoring the mental adultery Jesus condemned.

2. Can you stop masturbating? If not, you have elevated masturbation to god status in your life. God does not tolerate any pretenders to His throne. All idols must be removed.

3. Do you sense the Holy Spirit's conviction when you masturbate? Perhaps you are able to masturbate apart from fantasies. Maybe you can stop at will. But if you sense God's urging to stop, that's reason enough.

If you are trapped in the web of sexual fantasy and uncontrolled masturbation, there's hope. In chapter 13 we'll walk through the Steps to Freedom in Christ. Remember that "there is now no condemnation for those who are in Christ Jesus" (Romans 8:1). Pouring guilt and shame on yourself does not help you or anyone else, nor does this produce good mental health. What does help is receiving God's love and acceptance. God loves you, and He will not give up on you. You may despair in confessing again and again, but His love and forgiveness are unending.

God's Views on Homosexuality

God's view of homosexuality hasn't changed, even though society seems more accepting of this "alternate lifestyle." The New Testament places homosexuality in the same category with other sexual sins we must avoid: "Do not be deceived: Neither the sexually immoral nor idolaters nor adulterers nor male prostitutes nor homosexual offenders nor thieves nor the greedy nor drunkards nor slanderers nor swindlers will inherit the kingdom of God" (1 Corinthians 6:9,10).

Some argue, "But I was born this way. I have always had homosexual tendencies. I can't help it; this is the way God created me." But God did not create homosexuals. He created us male and female. Homosexuality is a lie. There is no such thing as a homosexual; there is only homosexual behavior. Think of it this way: God did not create child molesters, adulterers, or alcoholics. If someone can rationalize homosexual behavior, why can't another person rationalize adultery, fornication, child molestation, etc.?

One young man came to me (Dave) and asked my opinion about what Christian college he should attend if he wanted to get into counseling. But I soon discovered that he really wasn't seeking my wisdom on the Christian academic community. He was testing me to see if I could be trusted with a terrible secret.

He told me how he had accepted Christ as his Savior. And then he stated, "Dave, I'm a homosexual."

"No you're not," I replied.

He gave me a funny look and said, "Dave, trust me, I was there. I'm a homosexual."

"No, you're not!" I fired back. "I believe you are a child of God who struggles with sexual sin."

He sat silent for a moment, then replied, "I've never heard that before. That's hard to believe because I've felt this way all my life."

I asked him if he had ever been molested.

Without hesitating he said, "No, never."

I then asked him to tell me about his first sexual experience.

"Well, I was out behind the barn with two other guys and we had sex."

"How old were they?" I asked.

"One was eight and the other was nine."

"How old were you?"

"I was six."

I asked him to pray and ask the Lord if a six-year-old has a developed sex drive. He bowed his head for a moment, then he said, "I believe I might have been molested."

The lie that God had created him as a homosexual was destroyed. Certain events or influences in your past may have led you to homosexual behavior. But God never commands us to do something we cannot do. He has commanded us to "abstain" from homosexuality, and He has provided a way of escape. This way of escape is covered in chapter 13.

Our culture is bent on finding the ultimate sexual experience. But when they think they've found it, it satisfies only for a season, so the quest must continue. Unfortunately, Christians are influenced by the world's obsession with sex, and such a focus carries painful consequences.

Instead, we should be bent on finding the ultimate personal relationship: "Blessed are those who hunger and thirst for righteousness, for they will be filled" (Matthew 5:6). If you are willing to pursue the greatest of all relationships, one that every child of God can have with his Heavenly Father, you will be satisfied.

Purity Pointers

Read: 1 Thessalonians 4

Reflect: 1. Does God condemn sex? Why or why not? Why is the view that all sex is dirty or wrong incorrect? What does the word *abstain* mean when related to sexual issues?

2. What does it mean when a man and a woman become one flesh?

3. Give three reasons why sexual fantasy isn't meant for the Christian. How are fantasy and masturbation connected?

Respond: Dear Heavenly Father, I know that Satan has perverted sex, but You still show us Your perfect plan. Your way is the truth and that truth sets us free (John 8:32). Lord, I understand your design for sex and marriage and I choose to walk in Your ways. I choose to stay out of the darkness. I agree that You created us as sexual beings—male and female. Thank You for the wonderful gift of sex. Help me to save this gift for my mate. In Jesus' name I pray. Amen.

CHAPTER SIX

Why God Says Wait

I believe that teenagers today, empowered by the Holy Spirit, can do whatever they set their minds to. They can turn the tide by saying, "Sex is so great that it's worth waiting for."

—Greg Speck[1]

Everything we do and every choice we make has built-in consequences.

In early 1988 Charles and Diana, Prince and Princess of Wales, and some friends took a skiing trip to Switzerland. The shocking news came one afternoon of an avalanche in which one of the prince's lifelong friends was killed and another was seriously injured. It seemed sheer chance that the prince himself was not killed or hurt. How did it happen? A day or two later the press reported that the prince's group had chosen to ski on slopes that were closed to the public. Avalanche warnings were posted, but the group chose to go beyond the fence because, as one of them observed, that is where the optimum fun and excitement were to be found. Most likely, they found a branch of pleasure that was indeed more attractive. But it went beyond the margins of what was safe and wise. The result? Several broken worlds.

Like the prince and his party who chose to venture beyond the fences, all of us become curious and edge out to the fences, at least to see what is on the other side. Perhaps we want to see how far we can sneak away from God and not suffer the consequences.[2]

The same is true of our response to God's plan for sex and marriage. If we sow seeds of sexual immorality, we will reap a dark harvest. But if we stay within the boundaries of sexual purity in our relationships and marriages, we will reap God's benefits and blessings. Paul said it this way: "The one who sows to his own flesh shall from the flesh reap corruption, but the one who sows to the Spirit shall from the Spirit reap eternal life" (Galatians 6:8 NASB).

What are the consequences of sowing to the flesh in the area of sexual conduct? What kind of corruption is Paul talking about? First, there are physical consequences and secondly, relational consequences. Third, there are inward or spiritual consequences, which we will explore in chapter 10. Perhaps one or more of these consequences in your life has gotten your attention.

Why the Boundaries?

As I (Dave) began to travel with Josh McDowell it was the start of a sexual purity campaign called "Why Wait?" Time and time again I heard Josh say, "Within every negative commandment are two positive principles. God wants to *protect* something and God wants to *provide* for something." Like Charles and Diana you may see signs that say, "Do not enter" and think they are there just to restrict your fun. But in reality they were put there to protect you from harm and to lead you to the places where the safest and best fun can be had. Charles and Di may be royalty, but they still have to follow the same protective guidelines that govern you and me. And while it is true that you are a child of the most high God, if you step outside of His protective commandments, an avalanche of consequences will soon bury and smother your spiritual life and sometimes your physical life, as well.

Physical Consequences of Sexual Sin

Perhaps the most alarming fallout that results from ignoring God's design for sex is the physical consequences. Physical pain, the threat of disease and death, get our attention quickly.

Free sex isn't free. The potential price tag for sexual promiscuity in terms of health is staggering. Dr. Joe McIlhaney, a gynecologist, states that 30 percent of single, sexually active Americans have herpes. Another 30 percent have venereal wart virus. As many as 30 to 40 percent have chlamydia, which is rampant among teenagers and college students. Cases of gonorrhea and syphilis are increasing at an alarming rate.[3] Medical health experts insist that sexually transmitted diseases (STDs) are by far the most prevalent of communicable diseases.

The most frightening aspect of STDs is that they can be passed on without the carrier showing any symptoms. This is especially true for those who are HIV positive. Victims may go for years without showing signs of illness, unknowingly passing on the disease to their sexual partners who in turn pass it on to other unsuspecting victims. Without medical testing, a person cannot be sure that his or her sexual partner is free of STDs. Indeed, the partner may not even know he is infected. The rapid spread of STDs in our culture illustrates the chilling truth that a sexual encounter more often than not involves more than two people. If you have sex with a promiscuous person, as far as STDs are concerned, you are also having sex with every one of that person's previous sex partners, and you are vulnerable to the diseases carried by all of them.

The Relationship Consequences of Sexual Sin

Teenagers who have violated God's design for sex also pay a price in their future marriage relationships. We have counseled many women who, because of past illicit sexual experiences, can't stand for their husbands to touch them. Also, the mind is a powerful thing. It can store and recall an incredible amount of information. Memories of all of your past sexual experiences can return to haunt you. Your future spouse will not appreciate being compared to your other sex partners. Those reruns in the mind can give the enemy ammunition to use against you, but that type of accusation can't happen if he has nothing to draw from.

When you get married, your husband or wife may ask you about your sexual past. If your life is filled with sexual exploits your mate may struggle with trust issues. Every relationship needs trust. In fact, our relationship with Christ is based on trusting in and depending upon Him. Broken trust can be rebuilt in time, but it's much easier to simply keep your slate clean.

Another relationship issue is your virginity. You can only give it away once. While traveling with Josh McDowell I (Dave) heard him tell the story of a girl who was determined to save herself for her husband. Every day at school, her girlfriends would tease her and tell her that she could only be a woman if she had sex. Then they would brag about their own sexual experiences with their boyfriends. Finally, after she had heard enough of their bragging, she said, "Anytime I want I can become like you, but you can never again become like me!" That girl knew she could only give her virginity away once.

God doesn't want sex to be the dominant reason you're together as a couple. He wants you to know the difference between true love and sex. If you're sexually involved with another person before marriage your mind is focusing on getting sex, not developing the other person and the relationship.

The biggest relationship issue is, of course, with God. Sexual sin cuts off God's ability to bless you and lead you to the deep love and freedom that can be found in a pure relationship. Sexual sin forces God's hand of discipline. God wants you to protect your testimony so you will always be able to witness and share the love of Christ with others.

How Far Can I Go?

Often we are asked: "How far can I go physically and not get in trouble?" The question needs some adjustment: "How can I nurture purity?" Still, what about holding hands, kissing, French kissing, exploring someone's body, and sex? By now you should have a fairly good idea what God would say about some of these areas. Let's imagine for a moment that Jesus had dated and gotten married while He was on earth. Now, we know that wasn't His purpose—He came to save us from our sin. But if He had, what would Jesus do on a date? Hold hands? Kiss? More? Take a minute and put an "X" when you think Jesus would have gotten involved in the activities listed below.

What Would Jesus Do?

	First Date	Steady	Promised	Engaged	Married
Hold hands					
Kiss					
French kiss					
Explore					
All the way					

Figure 6

Do you know what you just did? You made rules for a Holy God—rules for the One who lives in you! Do you think your rules are more strict or more lenient than God's guidelines? When we ask that question, most young people say God's rules are more strict . . . but those same people are *really* tough on Jesus. They won't even let Him hold hands until He's married! The point is, if you follow God's guidelines in His Word and your own convictions for Jesus, you probably won't get into too much trouble.

God wants to provide you with the very best marriage and if possible, guilt-free memories. What some call freedom is really not, so be careful. If there is even a question in your mind that you shouldn't be doing what you're doing stop.

The Pressure Lines

Whenever you hear a pressure line from the guy or girl you're dating, it's not true love. True love never pressures. In fact, Jesus doesn't even pressure us to accept Him as Savior. Josh McDowell Ministries has a great T-shirt called, "I'm Not Doing It! (And Here's Why)":

1. I make lifelong decisions with my head, not my hormones.
2. If you care, you wouldn't dare.
3. Real men respect women.
4. I respect myself too much.
5. I'm saving it for marriage.
6. I don't owe it to anyone.
7. It's a thrill that could kill.
8. I need real love not cheap substitutes.
9. I want you to love me, not my body.
10. Real men don't act like animals.
11. Because God's plan is the best.
12. Because I want a real honeymoon.
13. Anybody can, but a man can wait.
14. Love is not an act; it's a commitment.

15. 55,000 Americans will get V.D. while doing it today.
16. What am I missing out on? Pregnancy? Guilt? Hurt? Disease?
17. AIDS is forever.
18. If you really love me, you can accept no.
19. I want to be accepted for who I am, not for what I have to give.
20. I'm not ready for junior yet.
21. It's just not worth it.
22. You don't want me, you want it.

If you are experiencing sexual pressure, you may want to reconsider the relationship. Remember Samson? Delilah's pressuring finally got the best of him. And it cost him a lot—his freedom and eventually his life. Don't play with fire. Get out of the tempting situation.

When It's Not Your Fault

In cases where persons were victims of severe sexual abuse such as rape or incest, their bodies were used as unwilling instruments of unrighteousness. Date rape is becoming more and more common. And even the best planned date can turn into a nightmare where victims become one flesh with their abusers. These acts of violent and abusive sex can pollute future marriage relationships. The good news is that people can be set free from the heartache and problems of such violations. They can renounce the unrighteous uses of their body, submit to God, resist the devil, and forgive those who abused them.

Sexual Sin Affects Many People

Sexual sin affects you and your family. The affair between King David of Israel and Bathsheba, wife of Uriah, is an example of what can happen when you ignore God's guidelines. David is called a man after God's own heart (Acts 13:22), but he had one dark blot on his life. First Kings 15:5 summarizes his life: "David had done what was right in the eyes of the Lord and had not failed to keep any of the Lord's commands all the days of his life—except in the case of Uriah the Hittite." And because of his moral failure, David's family paid a steep price. Let's take a look at his fatal steps and their tragic consequences.

"One evening David got up from his bed and walked around on the roof of the palace. From the roof he saw a woman bathing. The woman was very beautiful, and David sent someone to find out about her" (2 Samuel 11:2,3). There was nothing essentially wrong with Bathsheba's beauty and David's attraction to her. That's the way God made us. Someone might say, "Hey, didn't anybody ever tell you not to take a bath where people can see you?" Bathsheba shouldn't have bathed where others could see her, and David shouldn't have continued to look at her. David could have turned and walked away from the tempting sight and taken God's way of escape. But he didn't take it.

By the time David sent messengers to get Bathsheba, he was too far down the path of immorality to turn around. They slept together and she became pregnant. David tried to cover up his sin by calling Uriah, Bathsheba's husband, home from the battlefield to sleep with her. The pregnancy could then be attributed to him. But Uriah wouldn't cooperate, so David sent him back to the battle and arranged for his murder. Sin has a way of compounding itself. Cover-up, denial, and guilt make for a complex life. You have to keep track of each person you lied to and what each lie was.

After a period of mourning her dead husband, Bathsheba became David's wife. David lived under the guilt and covered his shame for nine months, apparently suffering physical consequences because of his sin. In Psalm 32:3 he describes his torment: "When I kept silent, my bones wasted away through my groaning all day long. For day and night your hand was heavy upon me; my strength was sapped as in the heat of summer."

David's troubles remind us of a D. L. Moody story we came across in Gordon McDonald's book, *Rebuilding Your Broken World*. Moody writes:

> Dr. Andrew Bonar told me how, in the Highlands of Scotland, sheep would often wander off into the rocks and get into places that they couldn't get out of. The grass on these mountains is very sweet and the sheep like it, and they will jump down ten or twelve feet, and then they can't jump back again and the shepherd hears them bleating in distress. They may be there for days, until they have eaten all the grass. The shepherd will wait until they are so faint that they cannot stand, and then they will put a rope around him, and he will go over and pull that sheep up out of the jaws of death.
>
> "Why don't they go down there when the sheep first gets there?" I asked.
>
> "Ah," he said, "they are so very foolish they would dash right over the precipice and be killed if they did." . . .

And that is the way with men; they won't go back to God till they have no friends and have lost everything. If you are a wanderer I tell you that the Good Shepherd will bring you back the moment you have given up trying to save yourself and are willing to let Him save you His own way.[4]

The Lord allowed plenty of time for David to come to terms with his sin. The king didn't confess, so God sent the prophet Nathan to confront him. God won't let His children live in darkness for long, because He knows it will eat them alive. "There is nothing concealed that will not be disclosed, or hidden that will not be made known" (Matthew 10:26).

Forgiveness and Consequences

David finally acknowledged his sins, both of which were capital offenses under the law. Then Nathan said, "The Lord has taken away your sin. You are not going to die. But because by doing this you have made the enemies of the Lord show utter contempt, the son born to you will die" (2 Samuel 12:13,14).

The Lord spared David, but his son by Bathsheba had to die. Why? God's law states, "I, the Lord your God, am a jealous God, visiting the iniquity of the fathers on the children, on the third and fourth generations of those who hate Me" (Exodus 20:5 NASB). Are we guilty of the sins of our parents? Absolutely not! Such was the belief in Israel, but it required a correcting word from the Lord in Ezekiel 18:4: "The soul who sins is the one who will die." Each of us is accountable for our own sin, but we are all affected by the sins of others.

You are not guilty for your parents' sins, but if your parents sin, judgment will fall upon you and your family according to the Mosaic covenant. Once a father has set himself against God, this desire to live for self will likely be passed to the next generation.

Additional judgment was meted out to David's household as a result of his sin. The prophet Nathan declared, "This is what the Lord says: 'Out of your own household I am going to bring calamity upon you'" (2 Samuel 12:11). The Lord's word was fulfilled. Two of David's sons, Absalom and Amnon, were involved in sexual immorality (see 2 Samuel 13 and 2 Samuel 16:22). Bathsheba's son died at birth. Amnon was later killed by his brother Absalom. And Absalom and David's other son Adonijah were both killed attempting to take the throne from David.

All this came upon David because he failed to turn away from the tempting sight of a woman bathing. How important it is to us and our loved ones to take every thought captive to the obedience of Christ (2 Corinthians 10:5).

Repentance Breaks the Chain

Repentance is God's answer to sin and self reliance, whether ours or our ancestors'. To repent means to have a change of mind about sin and to renounce it (Proverbs 28:13). But repentance is more than just admitting wrong doing. It is when we turn from sin and trust in God. It is when we choose to no longer hold iniquity in our hearts. We commit all we have and all we are to God. In this way we can become faithful stewards of everything God has entrusted to us (1 Corinthians 4:1,2).

Such a commitment may include our possessions, our activities, our families, and the use of our physical bodies, including sexual activity. As we renounce any previous use of these for the service of sin and then dedicate them to the Lord, we are saying that the god of this world no longer has any right over them. They now belong to God, and Satan can't have them or use them.

God forgives us when we repent, but He doesn't necessarily take away the consequences of our sin. If He did, we would soon learn that we could sin all we want and then turn to God for cleansing without any consequences.

David's sexual sin and murderous cover-up was tragic, and the consequences of sin in his own life and in the lives of his children were painful and longlasting. But his story has a happy ending. David repented of his sin and went on to shepherd Israel with integrity of heart and lead them with skillful hands (Psalm 78:72).

David's confession of sin in Psalm 51 is a model prayer for those who have violated God's plan for sex:

> Have mercy on me, O God, according to your unfailing love; according to your great compassion blot out my transgressions. Wash away all my iniquity and cleanse me from my sin. For I know my transgressions, and my sin is always before me. Against you, you only, have I sinned and done what is evil in your sight, so that you are proved right when you speak and justified when you judge. . . .
>
> Create in me a pure heart, O God, and renew a steadfast spirit within me. Do not cast me from your presence or take your Holy Spirit from me. Restore to me the joy of your salvation and grant me a willing spirit, to sustain me (verses 1-4,10-12).

But what if we sin and don't confess? What if we keep our sexual sins a secret instead of exposing them to the light? What kind of consequences can we expect?

In addition to the physical and relational consequences described in this chapter, continued sexual sin leads us down a dark path to the dead end of sexual bondage. Chapter 10 describes this process and prepares us for finding the way of escape. But first we're going to take a look at how we get headed down the wrong road to begin with.

Purity Pointers

Read: Read Psalm 51. Circle the verse in your Bible that speaks to you.

Reflect: 1. Why does God set up boundaries? What two things do we find in every commanment?

2. What are the physcal consequences of sexual sin? What are the relational consequences?

3. Write out your convictions about how far you're willing to go on a date. Would your parents like what you wrote? Would Jesus?

4. How does one's sexual sin affect others? How do you break the cycle?

Respond: Dear Heavenly Father, I understand that You put up boundaries in my life to protect me. I choose to stay within Your guidelines and I ask for Your protection. I don't want to reap any of the physical or relational consequences that come from sexual sin. Thank You for telling me that in Christ I am strong and I can do all things through Christ who strengthens me. In Jesus' name I pray. Amen.

> *For God did not call us to be impure,*
> *but to live a holy life.*
> *1 Thessalonians 4:7*

CHAPTER SEVEN

Detecting the Dangers in a Sex-Crazed World

> With Sex Ed, we show you how to do it,
> then we warn you not to do it—but we tell you
> if you decide to do it, to be careful, because it
> could kill you, make you sick, produce an
> unwanted baby. Talk about confusion!
> —Tony Campolo[1]

Jon's problems literally began in a dumpster. As a boy, that's where he came into contact with pornography for the first time. Curiously pawing through a trash bin on the military base where his father was stationed, Jon discovered more garbage than he had bargained for. He knew he should bury the dirty magazines and leave them there, but the tantalizing pictures captivated him. The hook was set.

As Jon entered puberty, the grip of pornography on

his mind strengthened. He became entranced with sexual fantasy and frequent masturbation. Jon's trips into the darker side of life also led him into experiments with alcohol, drugs, and sexual activity. Ironically, he retained the external image of a nice Christian boy. During high school he was active in Youth for Christ and involved in church, even though his parents did not attend.

When Jon turned 18, he enrolled in a Christian college. Even so, his uncontrolled desire to satisfy his sexual cravings led him into the hard-core realm of pornographic movies and his use of alcohol and drugs turned frightfully self-abusive. He abandoned his studies and his focus became wild parties and sexual escapades. To his embarrassment, Jon ended up flunking out of school.

Hoping to find direction for his life by following his father into a military career, Jon joined the Navy. But things only got worse. Drugs, alcohol, and pornography were everywhere. A random drug test uncovered Jon's drug problem, and he was repeatedly passed over for promotions.

Finally, lying in the base hospital after a job-related injury, Jon came to the end of himself. He cried out to the Savior he had only pretended to serve during his youth and turned his miserable life over to Him. The change was miraculous and instantaneous. His dependence on alcohol, drugs, and tobacco seemed to vanish, and his desire for pornography and illicit sexual encounters was suddenly gone.

But Jon's relief was short-lived. Three weeks later he happened upon a porno magazine in a rest room on the base. He yielded to the temptation and began a new cycle of sin, guilt, and frustration. He had let God down and shame overwhelmed him. He knew of no one he could talk to who would understand; he felt terribly alone. In despair, he beat himself up repeatedly with the thought, *If I had only left that garbage in the dumpster....*

Sex and Its Spell

I have the right to think for myself.
I have the right whether to have sex
   and with whom to have it.
I have the right to use protection when
   I have sex.
I have the right to buy and use condoms.
I have the right to express myself.
   —From the "Teenager's Bill of Rights"[2]

Jon's experience, the enslavement to lust and sinful habits is happening to people all around us. We have talked to hundreds of young people like Jon. Yet the world still shouts, "You have every right to sexual freedom." However, what they call freedom, Jon and countless others call a living hell.

You may not be as deeply involved as Jon, but the temptation confronts us all. The world says you have rights. The flesh shouts you have rights. The devil demands that you use your rights!

But we have been adopted into the family of the most high God, placed into a new and everlasting kingdom. The world has given us the "Teenager's Bill of Rights," but I wonder about our bill of rights in heaven. How does it read? God does not leave us ignorant and in the dark; He has given us His Word. He, too, has given us a Bill of Rights, the rights due every child of God—a right to purity and freedom!

The Christian's Bill of Rights—A Right to Purity

As a child of God I have the right to:

- keep my marriage bed pure and undefiled (Hebrews 13:4).
- flee immorality and say "no" to sin that would harm my body and my mind (1 Corinthians 6:18).
- abstain from sexual immorality and think of my future husband or wife and his or her interests (1 Thessalonians 4:3-5).
- present my body as a living and holy sacrifice to God (Romans 12:1).
- renew my mind and not be conformed to this world (Romans 12:2).
- lay aside the old self and the lust of desire and renew my mind (Ephesians 4:22,23).
- set my mind on the Spirit where there is life and peace, and avoid the flesh where there is death (Romans 8:5,6).
- fix my eyes on Jesus, the author and perfecter of my faith (Hebrews 12:2).
- let my mind dwell on whatever is true, honorable, right, pure, lovely, good, excellent, and anything worthy of praise (Philippians 4:8).
- keep seeking the things above, where Christ is seated at the right hand of God (Colossians 3:1).
- set my mind on the things above, not on the things that are on earth (Colossians 3:2).
- forget what lies behind and reach forward to what lies ahead, and press toward the goal for the prize of the upward call of God in Christ Jesus (Philippians 3:13,14).

- make a promise with my eyes not to look lustfully on a girl (Job 31:1).
- put on the Lord Jesus Christ, and make no provision for the flesh in regard to its lusts (Romans 13:14).
- encourage others and build them up (1 Thessalonians 5:11).
- walk by the Spirit and not carry out the desires of the flesh (Galatians 5:16).
- ask for and receive forgiveness and cleansing from all unrighteousness whenever I ask (1 John 1:9).
- escape any condemning charge against me because there is no condemnation, no punishment, for those who are in Christ (Romans 8:1).

Sexual sin is like Pandora's box. It opens you up to many other enslaving bondages as well. One study, comparing virgins to non-virgins, found that non-virgin girls were 2.5 times more likely to have used alcohol, 6.2 times more likely to have smoked marijuana, and 4.3 times more likely to have attempted suicide. Boys engaged in premature sex were 2.8 times more likely to have used alcohol, 6.3 times more likely to have smoked marijuana, and 2.7 times more likely to have attempted suicide.[3]

You may say, "You must be talking about unbelievers, especially when you mention becoming slaves to sexual sin."

No, we're not talking about unbelievers. The vast majority of those we counsel are evangelical Christians attending youth groups like yours and mine. Christians, young and old, are vulnerable to temptation, bad habits, and bondages related to sex.

When Jon first became involved with pornography,

he never imagined that it could have so much power over his life. But when he hit bottom, he knew that what began as a naive fascination had subtly enveloped him in its paralyzing tentacles.

The ultimate destination of even the most "innocent" or insignificant sexual temptation which remains unchecked is sexual bondage. None of the young men and women we have counseled ever intended for their sexual fantasies to control them. But, like the proverbial frog in the kettle of water, they were unaware that their secret fascination with pornography or sexual fantasy was slowly cooking them into submission.

Temptation leads to consideration, and consideration becomes a choice. After the choice is made the fantasy is fleshed out and becomes an action. As the action is repeated for some six weeks it becomes a habit. The habit becomes more entrenched until one's freedom to choose is lost. This is a stronghold. This is bondage.

Early in the process, the frog is able to jump out of the hot water. But after continually compromising with and acclimating to his potentially deadly environment, he becomes weak and unable to escape the trap (see Figure 7A).

Much of society labels this trap sexual addiction, but we call it sexual bondage. It is the condition of being under the control of sexual lust. We prefer the term bondage because of the biblical concept of being a slave to sin, which is at the root of the problem. The apostle Paul referred to himself as a bond-servant of Jesus Christ, and that's

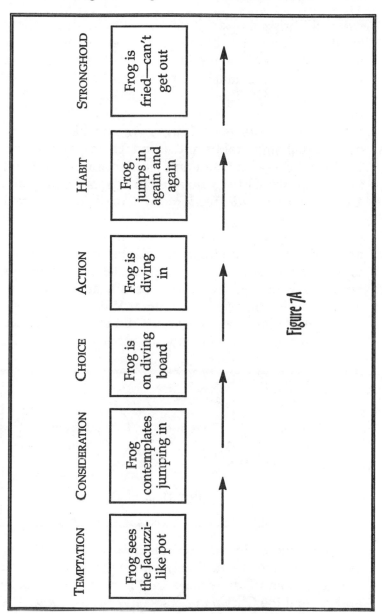

Figure 7A

TEMPTATION — Frog sees the Jacuzzi-like pot

CONSIDERATION — Frog contemplates jumping in

CHOICE — Frog is on diving board

ACTION — Frog is diving in

HABIT — Frog jumps in again and again

STRONGHOLD — Frog is fried—can't get out

what all Christians are called to be. Whenever we allow anything or anyone to have a greater hold over our lives than Christ, we become a slave to that thing or person. We have elevated another's power and authority over the power and authority of Christ in our lives, and that's sin.

As bond-servants of Christ, we can have victory over sexual immorality and bondage to sex because Christ has defeated Satan and sin. Since we can do all things through Christ who strengthens us (Philippians 4:13), we can find freedom in Christ from sexual bondage.

Some believe the answer to sexual addiction is therapy and behavior modification. We believe the answer to sexual bondage is repentance and faith. When we renounce what we have done as sin and choose to believe the truth, we are set free. What you believe determines how you behave, and how you behave determines how you feel—not the other way around!

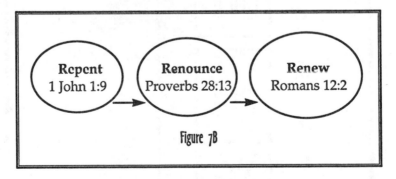

Figure 7B

The issue of losing control to sexual desires was clearly illustrated to me (Neil) when I was asked to visit a Marriage and Family class in a local secular college and present the Christian perspective on the topic. The class was made up of mostly girls with a few guys present.

One young man was clearly disinterested in my talk. He pulled his desk away from the group and read a book. He was listening, however, because he frequently interjected a vulgar noise in protest to my beliefs.

When I asked the class if they had any questions, one young woman asked, "What do Christians believe about masturbation?"

Before I could answer, the young man announced proudly so everyone could hear, "Well, I masturbate every day!"

The room fell silent as the other students anticipated my response. "Congratulations!" I said. "But can you stop masturbating?"

The young man was silent for the rest of the discussion. When class was dismissed, he waited for the other students to leave. As he strolled by me, he taunted, "So why would I want to stop?"

"I didn't ask if you wanted to stop," I replied. "I asked if you could stop, because if you can't, what you think is freedom is really bondage."

Freedom Versus Bondage

That's the issue: freedom versus bondage. If you are involved in sexually impure thoughts, deeds, or activities that are clearly in opposition to God's Word, stop. If you can't stop, then like Jon, you are in bondage to those thought patterns and activities and need to find your freedom in Christ. This book was written to help you succeed in those areas where all your self-determination, willpower, and counseling appointments have fallen short.

You may have picked up this book because you have a problem with nagging sexual temptations or bad habits. For example, you may have trouble staying away from novels with explicit sex scenes. You rationalized they were harmless entertainment as long as you didn't act out the temptations and fantasies that filled your mind. But now you're hooked on the stuff, and you find yourself craving even more risqué stories.

Maybe your biggest problem is with obscene movies and videos. You tell yourself that you watch them for the story while trying to ignore the steamy sex scenes. After all, it seems a lot of Christians attend movies featuring sex, violence, and nudity without consequences—but not so with you. You can't get enough of the stuff.

Or maybe you are secretly struggling with another unscriptural sexual behavior: a sexual relationship or an insistent fascination and attraction to homosexuality. You wish you could retrace every misstep that got you into this mess in the first place. For now, every act seems to drive you deeper into the darkness of your bondage.

But try as you might, you can't stop—and you don't know what to do about it. You long to be free, but you're afraid you are headed down the same dark, dead-end street that caused Jon so much pain and heartache.

If you really want to be free from your sexual bondages, we have good news for you. You can be free! Jon is living proof. When Jon was driven to the breaking point, he went to the mountains with some friends to pick up the pieces. One of Jon's friends gave him *The Bondage Breaker,* and he devoured it. He learned about the origin of the sexual strongholds which had ruled his life for so many years. Then in one three-hour session with God, Jon followed the Steps to Freedom found in *The Bondage Breaker* and in chapter 13 of this book. He renounced the strongholds in his life and dealt with a number of issues which had contributed to his bondage. Jon later said, "It was the most freeing time I have ever spent with God."

Purity Pointers

Read: Select five passages from the Christian's "Bill of Rights" and look them up.

Reflect: 1. Can you relate to Jon's experiences in this chapter? Do you feel like you're under the control of some sexual temptation or lust?

2. Do you ever feel like your sex drive is controlling you, like you can't say "no" to sexual sin? Have you ever felt like your sexual actions have caused you to compromise your walk with Christ? In what ways?

3. How does an evil consideration in your mind lead to a habit and a stronghold?

4. When a person's freedom to choose is gone, can that person ever be free again? What does Philippians 4:13 say about it? Why is it important to turn your back on sin and to renew your mind?

Respond: Strongholds are destructive mental habits burned into our minds over time, or possibly from traumatic experiences. Strongholds show up as ungodly personality traits and actions. Take a few moments to pray and ask God to reveal any sexual strongholds, habits, or actions that might have worked into your life.

Dear Heavenly Father, You have told us to put on the Lord Jesus Christ and make no provision for the flesh in regard to its lust (Romans 13:14). I ask You now to reveal any sexual strongholds or habits that I may have developed. I want to walk in the light and face the truth. May Your Holy Spirit lead me into all truth and may that truth set me free in Christ. In Jesus' precious name I pray. Amen.

> *Flee the evil desires of youth, and pursue righteousness,*
> *faith, love and peace, along with those who call on the*
> *Lord out of a pure heart.*
> *2 Timothy 2:22*

—Chapter Eight—

Pathways to a Dead End

> Lust is an overpowering desire to enter into the actual fulfillment of one's fantasy. When lust takes charge, normal restraints are removed. Personal reputation—blindness to the consequences—wrong is rationalized. There is a burning excitement to proceed, no matter what. Whoever reaches that point of no return *cannot* stop. The excitement reaches such a fever pitch, all restraint is tossed to the wind.
> —Charles R. Swindoll[1]

No one purposely sets out to become trapped in sexual bondage. First, a person faces the temptation to fulfill legitimate sexual needs in the world, the flesh, or the devil instead of in Christ. Each temptation brings him to the threshold of a decision. If he hesitates at the threshold instead of immediately taking the thought "captive to the obedience of Christ" (2 Corinthians 10:5 NASB), he increases his chances of yielding to that temptation.

Next, if he continues to yield to sexual temptation, he will form a habit. And if he exercises that habit long enough, a stronghold will be established in his mind. (See Figure 7A.) Once a stronghold of thought and response is entrenched in the mind, it becomes difficult to act in a way that's different from that pattern. Sexual bondage is a stronghold in the mind which causes you to act out your own desires rather than the will of God, even when you know and want to do otherwise.

If you or someone you know is gripped by sexual bondage, you must understand how you got involved in the first place in order to be set free. Identify the pathway which drew you into sexual bondage so you can renounce those impure thoughts and behaviors. And identify any persons who may have aided or encouraged you in this direction so you can forgive them.

In the process of teaching and counseling on this topic, we have discovered three broad pathways which lead to sexual bondage. The first pathway is sexual promiscuity—engaging in activities like sexual experimentation, fantasy, pornography, voyeurism, etc. The second pathway is sexual fascination with or exposure to homosexual influences. The third pathway is sexual abuse—hurtful experiences and influences from the past which can direct you to impure sexual behavior. In this chapter we will examine these three pathways and begin to understand how they lead the careless or unwitting victim into bondage.

It must be noted that few people find these pathways alone. The people in our past and present—parents, grandparents, brothers and sisters, other relatives, friends—exert tremendous influence in our lives. And sometimes these individuals push us in the wrong direction.

For example, a boy may be introduced to pornography by his father, who carelessly leaves magazines and videos lying around where the boy can find them. A male neighbor may befriend an unpopular teenage boy and influence him into homosexuality. A little girl may be molested by her uncle for years and grow up to be a sexually promiscuous teenager.

Maybe you were forced onto the pathway to sexual bondage when you were too young to understand or object. You may have been encouraged into immoral behavior by someone you trusted before you knew the act was wrong. "I'm hooked, and it's not my fault," you say.

It may be true that you are not fully responsible for the sin you got into. But you are responsible for choosing to remain there. As you explore the reasons behind your bondage, be encouraged that Jesus Christ has provided a way of escape. However, you can't blame anyone but yourself if you aren't free. You must take the exit God has provided. Part Three, "Freedom and Purity," and the Steps to Freedom in chapter 13 of this book will help you with that.

Playing with Fire

Andy grew up in a church-going family in the South. As a young boy he learned about pornography from his older brothers, who hid the magazines from their parents, but not from him. All through Christian elementary school and high school, Andy's secret fascination with pornography grew greater and greater. The books and magazines in his collection became increasingly more graphic. He restrained from physical sex because he knew it was clearly a sin, but sexual fantasies consumed his waking thoughts.

Sexual promiscuity is a major pathway to sexual bondage. We have heard variations of Andy's story from scores of men: pornographic magazines and movies leading to sexual fantasies, uncontrolled masturbation leading to experimentation, adultery, prostitution, or worse. We hear similar accounts from women who have been sucked into fantasy through their involvement with romance novels and dramas. Those who dabble in impure sexual thoughts and activities are playing with fire that may turn into a blaze called sexual bondage.

Just a Touch of Bondage

Many people head down the path of sexual experimentation believing they will never get sucked in too far. Some rationalize, "I'm not actually having sex, so no harm done, right?" Wrong! Fondling and exploring another person's body can cause you to lose your freedom.

We must understand how God views us and our bodies. You are not a plaything to be used to satisfy someone's sex drive. You're a temple of the Holy Spirit. First Corinthians 6:19,20 says, "Do you not know that your body is a temple [*naos*] of the Holy Spirit, who is in you, whom you have received from God? You are not your own; you were bought at a price. Therefore honor God with your body."

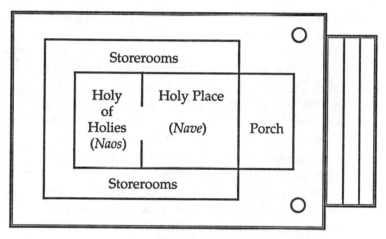

Whole Temple Area (*Iuron*)

Figure 8A—Biblical View of You

The Bible says you are a temple of the Holy Spirit and refers to you as the Holy of Holies, the *naos*. This is the place where only God dwelled. A high priest from the tribe of Levi was allowed to enter only once a year. Then, if he had even a single sin in his life that was undealt with, he died! When you accepted Christ you entered into the Holy of Holies—a place where God now dwells in His fullness and holiness. With that in mind, is sexual exploration of a Christian's body a big deal to God? First Thessalonians 4:4,5 reminds us "that each of you should learn to control his own body in a way that is holy and honorable, not in passionate lust like the heathen, who do not know God."

You may have read the book *The Lion, the Witch and the Wardrobe*. In chapter 3, Edmund finds his way into the land of Narnia and meets the terrible white witch. When she finds out that he is a human and from the outside world, she uses Turkish Delight to tempt him to bring his brother and sisters to her.

> At last the Turkish Delight was all finished and Edmund was looking very hard at the empty box and wishing that she would ask him whether he would like some more. Probably the Queen knew quite well what he was thinking; for she knew, though Edmund did not, that this was enchanted Turkish Delight and that anyone who had once tasted it would want more and more of it, and would even, if they were allowed, go on eating until they killed themselves.[2]

The point is clear. Touching where you shouldn't touch leads to more touching, which leads to more touching. First Peter 2:11 tells us, "Dear friends, I urge you, as aliens and strangers in the world, to abstain from sinful desires, which war against your soul." Abstain means "Don't go near! Keep away from it! Don't touch it!" Inappropriate touch is like Turkish Delight—you just want more and more. Remember where this cycle begins. With an unplanned date and not determining ahead of time what your boundaries are. When a tempting sexual thought comes into your mind tell it, out loud, to get!

The Lie of the "Alternate Lifestyle"

Thomas unintentionally discovered a pathway to

sexual bondage: homosexuality. He was raised by a domineering mother and a detached father he could never seem to please. He possessed a brilliant mind and found his acceptance in academics, graduating from college with a teaching degree. He found great happiness with Claudia, whom he married, and shared a faith in Christ. Together, they moved to a large city where Thomas began his career.

Thomas's life was full and satisfying. Claudia's love and acceptance warmed him. He enjoyed his work. He taught an adult Sunday school class at the church they attended. They were blessed by the birth of a daughter and, 14 months later, a son.

But the responsibility of parenthood brought unexpected pressures and conflict to Thomas's marriage, triggering old memories of his mother's dominance and his father's displeasure. The stress at home drove him deeper into his work. He spent increasing amounts of time away from Claudia doing more work. His relationship with God began to wane as he buried himself in his career.

That's when Thomas got involved with Aaron, whom he had once attempted to lead to Christ. As their friendship deepened, Aaron admitted to Thomas his years of inner turmoil over his sexual orientation. Thomas determined to guide his friend to the truth of God's Word.

Thomas went with Aaron into the seedy world of the gay bar scene, rationalizing his behavior as research in order to help his friend. But instead of pulling his friend out, Thomas was pulled in. In time, Thomas yielded to his first sexual encounter with a man.

Yet a conflict raged within Thomas. On one hand, he believed, though his belief was based on deception, that

God had created him to be a homosexual. On the other hand, he could not escape his understanding of God's Word on the subject of sexual purity.

No longer willing to continue the charade at home, Thomas left Claudia. Prompted by hurtful childhood experiences and clouded thinking, and after repeated steps down a pathway of fascination with homosexuality, he became trapped.

"But it wasn't his fault," some may argue. "Thomas came from a dysfunctional family. His father and mother provided a messed-up picture of male and female roles. His poor self-identity and behavior is the by-product of his environment."

It's true that other people may be partially or substantially responsible for setting us on the pathway to sexual bondage. And Satan takes advantage of these failures to establish strongholds of control in the lives of misused or abused children and youth. In the process of finding our freedom in Christ, we must deal with these people and experiences. However, we must try to focus, not on who is to blame, but on finding the way of escape. The individual in bondage is responsible to take steps to do that.

The Violation of the Innocent

A third pathway to sexual bondage is the experience of being the victim of another person's sexual sin. Many of these victims were molested as children by trusted adults. Some were victims of incest by parents, brothers, or sisters. Some were date-raped as teens or violently raped as adults. The common thread is that these victims were all sexually violated against their will.

Not all victims of sexual abuse end up in sexual

bondage. But a surprising number of the people we counsel at Freedom In Christ Youth Ministries admit some kind of past sexual abuse.

As with many victims, Melissa's memories of sexual abuse were at first blocked by the trauma she experienced. At one point, had you asked her if she were abused as a child, she would have said no. But her poor self-image and strange behavior signaled a deep, hidden problem. Melissa told us her story:

> I felt inadequate and unacceptable as a child. I avoided getting close to anyone, especially boys, fearing they would find out how terrible I was. Everyone seemed to relate to me in a sexual way. As a girl of six or seven, men whispered to me what they wanted to do to me when I got older. As I grew up, women seemed threatened by me, as if I intended to steal their husbands. This behavior only reinforced my belief that something was wrong with me, and everyone saw it. I had become a Christian as a young child, but I was convinced that God had picked me out to be tormented and abused.
>
> About the time I turned nine or ten, I began to experiment with masturbation. As a young teen I was shy and afraid of boys. I didn't have many friends. I rededicated my life to Christ at age 15. But as I left high school and entered college, I strayed into a few sexual involvements. I wanted to be loved and accepted, so I gave my body to these boys who just used and then discarded me. With or without sex, the boys rejected me. I felt dirty and trapped.

In her early twenties, Melissa married Dan, and
their physical intimacy opened a floodgate of memories
and nightmares about her clouded past. She dreamed
about her grandfather raping her. Gradually, the forgotten memories of her horrifying past came into focus.

Melissa remembered, at age two, being molested by
her grandfather. Then, as a young child, she was forced
to have sex and perform other atrocities with him. She
often woke in the middle of the night with severe
abdominal pains. An insightful doctor told Melissa's
mother she was being sexually abused. The mother
blamed Melissa's stepfather, brother, and uncle—everyone but her grandfather, the man who was doing it.

Melissa felt betrayed by the doctor for revealing her
"secret." Even though she felt it was wrong, she had
never considered telling anyone how Grandpa "loved"
her. She was confused. She loved her grandfather, but
she also prayed that God would kill him so that the
abuse would stop. When he did finally die in Melissa's
teenage years, she felt responsible and mourned him.
But the inner wounds he had inflicted continued to torment her for years.

Sexual abuse is a broad pathway to all kinds of
bondage, including sexual bondage. Studies show that
nearly half of all female children will experience some
form of sexual abuse before they reach their fourteenth
birthday.[3] Also 85 to 94 percent of sexual violations are
committed not by strangers, but by relatives, family
friends, neighbors, or acquaintances of the victim.[4]

Violation at such an impressionable age prompts distorted thinking in many victims of sexual abuse. Instead
of blaming the offender, who may be a relative the victim
desperately wants to trust and love, she blames God for
not protecting her. Others feel emotionally cut off from

God, saying, "I know God loves me, but my heart is numb to Him, because He all but violated me Himself by letting it happen."

The victim may also mistakenly blame herself for allowing such a thing to happen. As with Melissa, the thinking of many victims of abuse centers on self-blame which often leads to self-hatred and self-destructive behavior for "allowing" the abuse to occur. Rape victims often become their own victimizers as a result of intense feelings of shock, denial, fear, guilt, depression, and disorientation. These feelings may lead to suicide attempts, avoidance of the opposite sex, and nightmarish dreams.[5]

Like Melissa, many young victims of sexual abuse unconsciously protect themselves by blocking out the memories of these sad events. The intensity of the trauma overloads their minds and pushes those memories into a dark corner. This defense against the pain works well for children, but as they grow older it hampers their hold on reality. Many begin acting out their excessive need for love and protection, trying to satisfy this need with sex. This is why many who are caught in the web of sexual bondage cannot explain how they ended up there.

Melissa found a counselor who led her through the Steps to Freedom in Christ. She confessed the hurt, anger, and confusion that attended her history of sexual abuse. Her life and marriage were so radically changed that it's hard now to believe she is the same person.

Melissa now understands how much God loves her and realizes that her grandfather's sins can no longer touch her. She is free to enjoy life with the man who loves and accepts her completely. Her complete restoration from the bondage caused by sexual abuse is still in process as she walks in the truth of her freedom. And this same victory is available to all of God's children who desire release from bondage.

Perhaps while reading this chapter you have recognized a pathway which has led you into the sexually impure thought patterns and behaviors which now seem to control you. And you have possibly identified thoughts, events, and persons which have ushered you down this path to bondage. As important as these discoveries are, you yet need to get to the core of your sexual bondage. This issue is the subject of chapter 9.

If you are presently in an abusive situation at home or school, you need to cry out for help. Even if you love that person, you have every right to stop the madness. Go to your youth pastor, a trusted teacher, or an adult who cares about you for help.

Purity Pointers

Read: 1 Corinthians 6:19,20; 2 Corinthians 10:5; 1 Thessalonians 4:4,5; and 1 Peter 2:11.

Reflect: 1. What are the three pathways to sexual bondage? Why is it important to understand these pathways?

2. Could you personally identify with any of the pathways? If so, have you talked with a trusted adult about it?

3. Why does the "But it wasn't my fault" argument or "I come from a dysfunctional family" argument not help the person in bondage?

Respond: Dear Heavenly Father, You have made known to me the path of life. You will fill me with joy in Your presence, with eternal pleasures at Your right hand (Psalm 16:11). I confess to You, Lord, that I have not always gone down Your paths and I have chosen to go my own way. Please forgive me for straying away from You. I also know that many in my life have directed me down the wrong path. I choose to forgive them and walk in Your ways, Lord. In Jesus' name I pray. Amen.

CHAPTER NINE

The Seduction of Your Mind

> Probably the closest parallel to Satan's strategy to be found today in our contemporary society is used by the advertising business. A good advertiser can manipulate your thoughts and emotions from just about any state you could possibly be in right up to the point of believing you must have his product *now!*
> —Charles Stanley[1]

There is more behind sexual bondage than the bad influences of the world and the events or persons who have the power to lead you down the wrong path. We have an enemy. Satan has access to your life story; he knows what pathways you have traveled. It would be so much easier if the strongholds in our minds were simply the result of all the garbage we fed into our computer brains when we were growing up. If that were the case, we could simply reprogram our minds through Bible study, good counseling, and more education. Certainly, those three things are a big part of breaking down bondages. But there is more to the story. We have a spiritual enemy who acts like a computer "virus" seeking to gum up the whole works.

Thoughts in Your Mind

We have been warned in 1 Timothy 4:1, "The Spirit clearly says that in later times some will abandon the faith and follow deceiving spirits and things taught by demons." It may alarm you to realize that Satan and his cohorts can put thoughts into our minds. How does this work? Does Satan sit down with us face to face and say, "Now listen. This is Satan speaking, and this is what I want you to do . . ."? No, he is much more clever than that. He tries to make *his* thoughts appear as *our* thoughts!

For example, right after Jesus had congratulated Peter for saying to the Lord, "You are the Christ, the Son of the living God," He had to correct His disciple. Why? Jesus had just told the disciples He would have to suffer and die. Peter took the Lord aside and told Him He was wrong—He would not have to die. Jesus looked straight at Peter and said, "Get behind Me, Satan!"

Do you think Peter would have tried to talk Jesus out of going to the cross if he knew the idea was not his, but Satan's? Peter must have thought, to himself, *I'm glad I thought of that!* and proceeded to tell Jesus his great idea. You can read the whole story in Matthew 16.

The point is that Satan is capable of putting thoughts into our minds, and then making us believe the thoughts originated with us! And when the enemy puts thoughts in our minds, he often uses the first-person tense. For example, Satan doesn't say, "You're stupid!" You would wonder where that voice came from. He's smarter than that. He disguises his thoughts as your own selftalk, like, "I'm so stupid."

Why does the devil plant these thoughts in our minds? In order to turn us away from following Christ! The following story is one example of his master plan.

The Pimp in Your Mind

Before he met Christ, Rick's life was an endless quest for intimacy. As a child, he was sexually abused by his grandmother. After his father committed suicide, his mother became involved in religious activities, devoting her life to ministry. So as a young man Rick embarked on a desperate search to fill the hole which the sins of others had left in him. Even after his marriage to Emily, his college sweetheart, he kept trying to cover his bitterness and hurt with other sexual encounters, work, and the approval of others, but without success. Emily lost patience and left him.

Then, one day while listening to a tape by a Christian speaker, Rick fell to his knees and asked Jesus to save him from himself and from the sin that never delivered what it promised. He and Emily were reconciled and eventually had four children. They seemed to be the model Christian family.

But deep inside, Rick was still taunted by the lie that sex, food, work, and other people could meet his needs more fully than Christ. He listened to that lie and fell back into his old patterns of immorality. He became sexually involved with numerous partners while continuing to play the role of Christian husband and father. He lived a double life in constant turmoil.

Finally, Rick confessed everything to his family and entered a 12-step program for his addictions. But Emily was crushed and told him not to return home. Then she divorced him.

For years Rick rode a spiritual and emotional roller coaster. Conviction would drive him to break off his relationships and return to the Lord. Then depression or problems would hit, and he would seek the familiar ways of escape: illicit sex, food, success. He felt powerless to control his behavior. He recalls: "The 'pimp' in my mind repeatedly promised me fulfillment if I would only prostitute myself one more time. But he never fulfilled his promise. My sexual addiction was destroying me from the inside out."

Rick's mother invited him to attend a Freedom In Christ Conference. He consented to go, but during the first evening of the conference he was harassed by sexual fantasies prompted by Satan, the pimp in his mind. However, one biblical statement did sink in and give him hope: "So if the Son sets you free, you will be free indeed" (John 8:36). Rick says, "I knew I wasn't free. I was powerless to stop the fruitless search for fulfillment and satisfaction in sex, food, and work."

Rick's mother set up a freedom appointment for Rick and me (Neil) to meet privately during the conference. He continues his story: "I knew while driving to the meeting that something was about to happen. My heart felt like it was going to explode. There was a war raging within me.

"Neil listened quietly as I shared my story, then he said in a calm voice, 'Rick, I believe you can be free in Christ.'

"As Neil led me through the Steps to Freedom in Christ, I could hear the pimp's insistent lies in my mind. The inner battle was intense, but I was ready for the shackles to be broken. So I repented of my sin, renounced all the lies I had believed, renounced every sexual use of my body as an instrument of unrighteousness, and forgave all those who had offended me. As I did, peace began to roll in and drown out 37 years' worth of lies. I heard holy silence. The pimp was gone and, praise God, I was free."

Since that conference, Rick has experienced a genuine and growing relationship with his Heavenly Father. He has stopped watching TV and attending movies, two activities which had played a large part in feeding his impurity. He now has an unquenchable desire to study the Bible and pray. And he has remained sexually pure. "It's a miracle!" Rick says. "I have been set free from that lying pimp in my mind."

We believe that every child of God can experience the kind of freedom Rick has found. Jesus broke the power of sin on the cross by defeating the god of this world—Satan, the lying pimp Rick talked about. To appropriate and retain your freedom, you must understand the continuing work of the evil one. He is the lying deceiver at the core of sexual bondage.

Enemy in the Garden

God's plan for the sexual life and health of His human creation has been clear since the beginning.

> The Lord God said, "It is not good for the man to be alone. I will make a helper suitable for him." . . . So the Lord God caused the man

to fall into a deep sleep; and while he was sleeping, he took one of the man's ribs and closed up the place with flesh. Then the Lord God made a woman from the rib he had taken out of the man, and he brought her to the man. The man said, "This is now bone of my bones and flesh of my flesh; she shall be called 'woman,' for she was taken out of man." For this reason a man will leave his father and mother and be united to his wife, and they shall become one flesh. The man and his wife were both naked, and they felt no shame (Genesis 2:18,21-25).

God created Adam in His image, breathed life into him, and Adam became spiritually and physically alive. Something was missing, however. It wasn't good for Adam to be alone; he needed a suitable helper. None of the animals God had created could adequately fulfill Adam's need. So God created Eve from Adam's rib. The couple was naked and unashamed. There was nothing obscene about their naked bodies. Their sexual relationship was not separated from their intimate relationship with God. There was no sin and nothing to hide, so Adam and Eve had no reason to cover up.

The purpose and responsibility of this first couple was to "be fruitful and increase in number; fill the earth and subdue it" (Genesis 1:28). They were given a tremendous amount of freedom as long as they remained in a dependent relationship with God. They had a perfect life and could have lived forever in God's presence. All their needs were provided for.

But Satan and evil were also present in the universe. The Lord had commanded Adam and Eve not to eat from the tree of the knowledge of good and evil or they would die (Genesis 2:17). But Satan twisted God's command and tempted the couple through the same three channels of temptation that exist today: "the lust of the flesh and the lust of the eyes and the boastful pride of life" (1 John 2:16 NASB). Deceived by the craftiness of Satan, Adam and Eve defied God, ate of the forbidden fruit, and declared their independence from God.

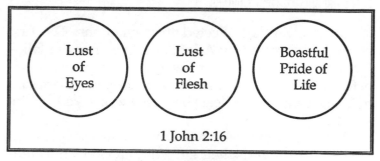

Figure 9A—The Channels of Temptation

At that moment, Adam and Eve died spiritually, meaning that their intimate relationship with God was broken. In time, they also died physically, which is also a consequence of sin (Romans 5:12). But in the coming years, their perfect life in the garden was ruined by their sin. No longer innocent and without shame, "the eyes of both of them were opened, and they realized they were naked; so they sewed fig leaves together and made coverings for themselves . . . and they hid from the Lord God among the trees of the garden" (Genesis 3:7,8).

1. The Fall Darkened Their Minds

The fall affected Adam and Eve's daily life in many

ways. First, it darkened their minds. In trying to hide from God, they revealed that they had lost a true understanding of God. Can you imagine trying to hide from God, who is present everywhere?

They had suffered serious brain damage. They had lost their understanding because they were separated from the life of God (Ephesians 4:18).

2. The Fall Affected Their Emotions

Second, the fall affected their emotions. The first emotions expressed by Adam and Eve after the fall—fear and guilt—had never been part of their existence before. When God came looking for the pair, Adam said to Him, "I was afraid [fear] because I was naked [guilt]; so I hid" (3:10).

The fear of exposure has driven many people from the light that reveals their sin. Without God's unconditional love and acceptance, they are forced to run from the light or discredit its source. Unable to live up to God's eternal standards of morality, they now face the prospect of living in guilt and shame or, like Adam, blaming someone else (Genesis 3:12).

3. The Fall Affected Their Choices

Third, the fall affected Adam and Eve's will. Before they sinned, they could only make one wrong choice: to eat from the forbidden tree of the knowledge of good and evil. Every other choice they could make in the garden was a good choice. However, because Adam and Eve made that one bad choice, they were afterwards confronted every day with many good and bad choices—just as we are today. We can choose to yield or not yield to a variety of temptations presented to us by the world, the flesh, and the devil. It is the pattern of consistent wrong choices in the area of sexual sin that leads individuals into sexual bondage.

Because of sin, we are totally helpless and hopeless to escape sexual bondage. In truth, without God, no person can live a moral life or withstand the conviction of His perfect light. "Everyone who does evil hates the light, and will not come into the light for fear that his deeds will be exposed. But whoever lives by the truth comes into the light, so that it may be seen plainly that what he has done has been done through God" (John 3:20,21).

Walking in the Light

The first step of recovery for anyone in sexual bondage is to come out of the darkness of hiding and face the truth in the light. Many people have told us that they want to get out of sexual bondage because they are tired of living a lie. And bondage to sex is one of the easiest bondages to lie about. For example, the effects of food addiction (either overeating or anorexia and bulimia) show up quickly in a victim's physical appearance. Drug or alcohol addiction is noticeable within a couple of years. But there are no obvious clues to sexual bondage, unless it surfaces in the form of a sexually transmitted disease. It can remain a private nightmare for a lifetime unless it is brought into the light and dealt with. "He who conceals his sins does not prosper, but whoever confesses and renounces them finds mercy" (Proverbs 28:13).

A Rebel Takes Control

At the root of the world's problem with sin and

bondage is Satan. When Adam and Eve sinned, Satan took over their role as ruler over the earth and became the rebel holder of authority. Satan tempted Jesus, offering Him the kingdoms of the world if He would bow down and worship him (Luke 4:6). Jesus didn't dispute Satan's claim to earthly authority and even referred to him as "the prince of this world" (John 12:31; 14:30; 16:11). Paul called Satan "the prince of the power of the air" (Ephesians 2:2 NASB). As a result of Adam and Eve's fall, "the whole world is under the control of the evil one" (1 John 5:19).

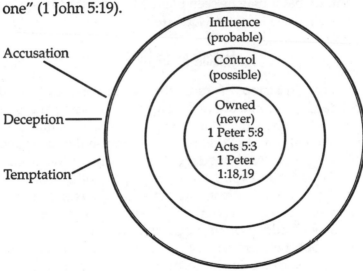

Figure 9B—Degrees of Vulnerability

The good news is that God's plan of salvation was underway immediately after Satan wrestled authority from Adam and Eve. The Lord cursed the serpent and foretold the downfall of Satan (Genesis 3:14,15), which was accomplished by Christ on the cross. Ultimate authority in heaven and earth now belongs to Him. Satan's days of authority on earth are numbered. Because we are related to Adam and Eve, all of us were born spiritually dead and were subject to the authority of the prince of this world. But when we received Christ, we were transferred from Satan's kingdom to God's kingdom (Colossians 1:13; Philippians 3:20,21). Satan is still the ruler of this world, but he is no longer our ruler; Jesus Christ is.

However, as long as we live in Satan's world, he will try to deceive us into believing that we belong to him. Even as members of Christ's kingdom we are still vulnerable to Satan's accusations, temptations, and deceptions. (See Figure 9B.) "But I am afraid that just as Eve was deceived by the serpent's cunning, your minds may somehow be led astray from your sincere and pure devotion to Christ" (2 Corinthians 11:3). If you give in to his tricks, Satan can influence your thinking and behavior. And if you remain under his influence long enough, Satan can control you in those areas where you have given him the right.

Satan's Primary Weapon

One of Satan's primary weapons for ruining relationships is sexual impurity. More young Christian lives are destroyed because of sexual misconduct than for any other reason. People who are in secret sexual bondage have no joy in friendships and dating. And facing marriage and ministry seem impossible. We hear so many accounts of couples who had sex one night only to end the relationship the next day. On the other hand, a person who seeks out a life of purity has a great start for a possible future in both marriage and ministry.

And dating and friendships are more manageable.

Satan is still in the business of selling his perversions of God's design for sex and marriage. In the next part we're going to take a look at how a habit forms. But best of all, we're going to go through the Steps to Freedom in Christ. Things can be different for you!

Purity Pointers

Read: Colossians 1:13; Philippians 3:20

Reflect: 1. How do we know that Satan can put thoughts into our minds? How does he trick us into believing they are our thoughts?

                   2. How were we affected by Adam and Eve's sin in the garden? What did Satan gain?

                   3. What are the three channels of temptation talked about in 1 John 2:16?

Respond: Dear Heavenly Father, I know that like Adam and Eve I can be deceived by the serpent's cunning lies and that my mind may somehow be led astray from my sincere and pure devotion to Christ. By the Power and the Blood of the Lord Jesus Christ I demolish any arguments and every pretension that sets itself up against me and the truth of God, and I choose to take captive every thought and make it obedient to Christ. In Jesus' name I pray. Amen.

PART THREE

Freedom
and
Purity

> *For though we live in the world, we do not*
> *wage war as the world does.*
> *2 Corinthians 10:3-5*

—CHAPTER TEN—

How a Habit Forms

A stronghold is a mindset impregnated with hopelessness that causes one to accept as unchangable something known to be contrary to the will of God.

—Ed Silvoso[1]

Joe notices a new girl in his chemistry class, Mary. She's beautiful. Joe feels a rush of emotion just looking at Mary. When Mary returns his glance with a smile, Joe's face flushes and his heart races with excitement. He's never felt so high. When the bell rings and Mary walks out of class, Joe's feelings decline. It's over for now, but he liked what he felt. He can't wait to see Mary again and repeat the sensational high.

All week long Joe watches Mary in class with the same wonderful, exciting results. Now, Joe is a nice Christian boy, and he has his standards of sexual purity. He has Mary's best interests at heart. But Joe craves more of that glorious high. So he invites Mary on a date (without becoming friends first).

Riding in the car with Mary brings a tremendous rush. When she innocently reaches over and touches his leg, Joe almost flies out the top! They hold hands and end the date with a light hug. Joe thinks he's in love. So far, so good. He has not compromised his standards . . . much. But he begins to imagine what it might feel like if they went a little farther.

Before long, a hug and then a kiss don't give Joe the same rush they first did. To have the same euphoric experience, Joe must become a little more adventurous. However, going farther means he must compromise his moral convictions a little more. Joe is more free with his hands during their passionate good night kisses. When he's alone he begins to fantasize about touching and kissing other parts of Mary's body.

At first stepping over the line was worth it to Joe because of the immediate gratification. But as the euphoria declines, Joe's conscience kicks in with twinges of guilt and shame. So he quickly overcomes these uncomfortable feelings with more sexual thoughts and experiments. Each new compromise brings greater conviction, which introduces greater compromise. At this point, Joe is caught in a downward spiral.

Like a drug, seemingly harmless injections of euphoria wear off and call for greater doses. As lust grows, more experience is required to quench it. But it can't be satisfied. The more a desire is fed, the larger it grows.

Normal sexual experiences don't seem to bring the

euphoria that a simple touch once did. So other experiences must be tried to get that same high. Self-centered thinking begins to take control. The conviction to not violate another's conscience or moral boundaries is replaced by "How far can I get her to go?" As the decline continues, a sexual habit brings an increasing sense of dependence on the experience. The pleasurable act becomes a means of releasing stress and tension. There is an increased tolerance for sin as the mind is repeatedly filled with pornographic images and actual experiences.

Many of those caught in this downward spiral begin to withdraw from people and from God. If left unchecked, this spiral eventually opens the door to sexually transmitted diseases and perhaps death. Fear and danger replace love and trust in the search for greater sexual highs.

A Spiritual Battle

We fight the spiritual battle in the area of sexual purity on many fronts, so be aware that in moments of temptation, every time you choose to follow lustful desires instead of God's plan for sexual purity, you are moving toward a lifestyle of sexual impurity. And Satan, the "father of lies" (John 8:44), couldn't be more pleased.

God brings judgment upon those who will not honor Him. He gives them over to their degrading passions. When the church at Corinth condoned an incident of sexual perversion, Paul instructed them, "Hand this man over to Satan, so that the sinful nature may be destroyed and his spirit saved on the day of the Lord" (1 Corinthians 5:5).

God graciously provides a way of escape through Christ. No matter where a person is in his or her flight from the truth into darkness, there is a way out. The serial rapist and murderer on death row is just as welcome to God's forgiveness and deliverance as is the child who lies about stealing a cookie. In God's economy, sin is not measured in quality or quantity. Kay Arthur, in her book *Lord, I Need Grace to Make It*, tells the true stories of William Cowper and John Newton. Kay writes:

> Could someone who had two mental breakdowns and attempted suicide three times ever be used of God?
>
> Yes, because the grace of God had appeared to all men.
>
> But if after he knew God and had experienced the Spirit-filled life, he then became depressed for over a year, could he ever again testify of the sufficiency of Jesus Christ?
>
> Yes, because the grace of God had appeared to all men.
>
> But could a man who had raped slaves, mocked the gospel, and tried to destroy the faith of others ever hope to know God, let alone be used of Him?
>
> Yes, because there was grace . . . sufficient for all his sin.
>
> But what if after he had believed in Christ Jesus, he was once again conquered by the lust of his eyes? What if he raped again? Could he ever hope to know the power of Christ upon his life, to know the benefits of His mercy?

Could he ever hope to be used by God? Or must he be condemned to a life without purpose?

No, for the grace of God has appeared to all men.

Neither William Cowper, the man who battled depression, nor John Newton, the rapist, would be denied renewed intimacy with God. God's grace covered all their sins and His grace would tie them to His love. Grace would forever anchor them within the veil of His presence.

William Cowper wrote: "There is a fountain filled with blood, drawn from Emmanuel's veins and sinners plunged beneath that flood, lose all their guilty stains." His cry in the hymn "O' for a Closer Walk with God," would become the melodious plea of generations to follow. Cowper would become one of the major poets of England in the latter half of the eighteenth century.

Cowper's life touched generations as a result of God's amazing grace. He learned of God's grace through the testimony of the slave trader John Newton in the book *Out of the Depths*. Cowper was convinced that God's salvation could never reach him. But he began to believe otherwise through the friendship of the one who wrote, "Amazing grace, how sweet the sound that saved a wretch like me." God would reach William Cowper with His grace. Grace, grace marvelous grace coming down from the Father above. Amazing grace.[2]

Is there hope for those who have gone too far? Can we repent of our sinful ways and return to God? Of course we can. If we understand and choose to believe our position in Christ, we can always have victory over sin.

Strongholds in the Mind

In order to battle sexual bondage in our lives, we must understand how strongholds are built in the mind. A stronghold is an established, habitual pattern of thinking and behaving against which the individual is virtually powerless to choose or act. Formation of these strongholds occurs in two ways, often beginning early in life.

The first avenue in which sexual bondage can come to us is through the experiences in our lives, such as families, friends, churches, neighborhoods, jobs, etc. As children, our attitudes and actions were partially shaped by these influences. For example, friends may have shared their pornographic magazines with you and encouraged you into a fascination with pornography. Or if a relative sexually abused you as a child, this experience will have influenced your thinking and behavior.

Environment is one of the determining factors in our human development. Still, two children can be raised in the same home by the same parents, eat the same food, play with the same friends, attend the same church, and still respond differently to life. We are individual expressions of God's workmanship (Psalm 139:13,14; Ephesians 2:10).

The second great contributor to the development of strongholds in our minds is traumatic experiences. Whereas other experiences influence our minds over time, one traumatic experience can be instantly burned into our memory because of its intensity. For example, one encounter with a nest of hornets may leave a child with a deep fear of all flying, stinging insects on into adulthood. Perhaps you were raped. Or maybe your parents were divorced, or one of them died suddenly. All of these traumatic experiences are stored in our memory bank and influence our thinking.

As we struggle to reprogram our minds against the negative input of past experiences, we are also confronted daily with an ungodly world system. Paul warned us, "Do not conform any longer to the pattern of this world" (Romans 12:2). As Christians we are not immune to worldly values; we can allow them to affect our thinking and behavior. But Paul insisted, "Don't let them influence you!" He also instructed, "See to it that no one takes you captive through hollow and deceptive philosophy, which depends on human tradition and the basic principles of this world rather than on Christ" (Colossians 2:8).

Since we live in this world, we will continuously face the temptation to conform to it. It is not a sin to be tempted. If it were, Christ was the worst sinner who ever lived, because He was "tempted in every way, just as we are yet was without sin" (Hebrews 4:15). We sin when we consciously choose to give in to temptation.

All temptation is Satan's attempt to get us to live our lives without God, to walk according to the flesh rather than according to the Spirit (see Galatians 5:16-23). Satan knows exactly which buttons to push. He knows your weaknesses and your family history.

Each temptation begins with a seed thought planted in our minds by the world, the flesh, or the devil himself. Since we live in Satan's world, we must learn how to stand against the temptations he throws at us. Since the media uses sex to entertain and to sell everything from beer to deodorant to toothpaste to cars, we are constantly bombarded with seed thoughts perverting God's plan for sex. Many people are easily tempted with sexual sin without much prompting from the external world, because they have programmed so much junk into their minds through TV, movies, books, and magazines.

One reason sexual strongholds are so difficult to overcome is because once they take hold in the mind, the mental pictures are always there for instant recall. An alcoholic can't get drunk by fantasizing about a bottle. A drug addict can't get high by imagining himself snorting cocaine. A habitual overeater isn't soothed thinking about a giant chocolate cake. But some victims of sexual bondage can get a rush, a high without any new pictures in the mind to draw from.

If when tempted we continue to make wrong choices, a habit can be formed in about six weeks. If the habit goes on, a stronghold will be developed in the mind.

Sexual strongholds are the dark dead end of sexual temptation, sexual sin, and impure habit patterns. You may know about God's plan of sexual purity and even agree with it. But, try as you might, you can't conform to it.

So if God's Word so clearly and strongly commands us not to live in sexual bondage, why don't we just obey God and stop doing what He forbids? Because understanding what we are doing wrong does not give us the power to stop doing it. Paul declared, "If a law had been given that could impart life, then righteousness would certainly have come by the law. But the Scripture declares that the whole world is a prisoner of sin"

(Galatians 3:21,22). The law is powerless to take away the problem. Something more is needed. Even more discouraging is Paul's statement, "The sinful passions aroused by the law were at work in our bodies" (Romans 7:5). The law not only can't help us do right, it actually has the capacity to provoke what it is trying to prohibit. Forbidden fruit always appears more desirable. Laying down the law does not remove sinful passions. The abstinence message alone doesn't work. The core problem is not people's behavior, but their basic nature.

If we try to live a righteous life externally when we are not righteous internally, we will become "whitewashed tombs, which look beautiful on the outside but on the inside are full of dead men's bones and everything unclean" (Matthew 23:27). The focus must be on the inside: "For from within, out of men's hearts, come evil thoughts, sexual immorality, theft, murder, adultery, greed, malice, deceit, lewdness, envy, slander, arrogance, and folly. All these evils come from inside and make a man `unclean'" (Mark 7:21-23).

If trying harder to live in sexual purity doesn't work, what will? Two verses in the Bible state what must happen in order for us to live righteously in Christ: "The reason the Son of God appeared was to destroy the devil's work. No one who is born of God will continue to sin, because God's seed remains in him" (1 John 3:8,9). If you will ever be set free from sexual bondage and be able to walk in that freedom, your basic nature must be changed, and you must have a means for overcoming the evil one.

For the Christian, these conditions have already been met. God has made us partakers of His divine nature (2 Peter 1:4) and provided the means by which we can live in victory over sin and Satan.

Before Christ, we were dead in our sins and subject to the control of Satan.

The following words describe us:

> You were dead in your trespasses and sins, in which you formerly walked according to the course of this world, according to the prince of the power of the air, of the spirit that is now working in the sons of disobedience. Among them we too all formerly lived in the lusts of our flesh, indulging the desires of the flesh and of the mind, and were by nature children of wrath (Ephesians 2:1-3 NASB).

But a change took place at salvation. Paul wrote, "You were once darkness, but now you are light in the Lord" (Ephesians 5:8). Our old nature in Adam was darkness; our new nature in Christ is light. We have been transformed at the core of our being. We are no longer "in the flesh"; we are "in Christ." Paul wrote, "Those who are in the flesh cannot please God. However you are not in the flesh but in the Spirit, if indeed the Spirit of God dwells in you" (Romans 8:8,9 NASB).

Before we became Christians we were under the rule of the god of this world, Satan. But at salvation God "rescued us from the dominion of darkness and brought us into the kingdom of the Son he loves, in whom we have redemption, the forgiveness of sins" (Colossians 1:13,14). We no longer have to obey the evil prompting of the world, the flesh, and the devil. We "have been given fullness in Christ, who is the head over every power and authority" (Colossians 2:10). We are free to obey God and walk in righteousness and purity.

We cannot fix the failure and sin of the past, but by the grace of God we can be free from it. God's Word promises, "If anyone is in Christ, he is a new creation; the old has gone, the new has come!" (2 Corinthians 5:17). Furthermore, we are seated with Christ in the heavenlies, far above Satan's authority (Ephesians 2:4-6; Colossians 2:10,11), and so the way is paved for us to live in victory and freedom over sin and bondage. But we have a responsibility. We must believe the truth of who we are in Christ and change how we walk as children of God to conform to what is true.

Paul writes in Ephesians 1:18,19, "I pray also that the eyes of your heart may be enlightened in order that you may know the hope to which he has called you, the riches of his glorious inheritance in the saints, and his incomparably great power for us who believe." We already share in Christ's inheritance, and we already have the power to live victoriously in Christ. God has provided these glorious benefits for us. The problem for most Christians in bondage is that they just don't see it.

Purity Pointers

Read: Ephesians 2:1-10

Reflect: 1. What is a spiritual stronghold? How do habits form? What did you learn from Joe in this chapter?

2. How is sexual sin and its cravings different from a craving for alcohol or drugs? Can we keep secrets from God?

3. Why does one sexual experience often

lead to other moral compromises? Can God break the cycle in us of constant desire for new sexual highs? What did you learn from the life of William Cowper and John Newton?

Respond: Dear Lord, thank You that I can have victory over sin when I choose to trust in You and what You said about me and my position in Christ. I know sexual strongholds are dangerous, so I ask You to reveal to me any way that I might be compromising my sexual purity. I don't want any bad habits or strongholds to form in my life. Thank You for always loving me and telling me the truth in love. In Jesus' name I pray. Amen.

*Do you not know that your body is a temple
of the Holy Spirit, who is in you, whom you
have received form God? Your are not your own.
(1 Corinthians 6:15-19).*

—CHAPTER ELEVEN—

You're Alive!

The simple insight of renouncing every sexual use of my body and mind outside of marriage proved so helpful when I first heard it. As I asked Christ to bring to my mind each instance of sexual sin, three vivid memories popped into my thoughts. Each one was, I now believe, a foothold Satan and his demons used to form a stronghold in my mind. Renouncing each one led to greater freedom and joy than ever before.

—Dr. Charles Mylander[1]

What do you believe about who you are in Christ? The Bible says of us, "For as he thinks within himself, so he is . . ." (Proverbs 23:7 NASB). Satan's deceptions and lies have caused a lot of people to be destroyed because of a lack of knowledge (Hosea 4:6). Your choice to believe God or Satan is the difference between freedom and bondage. Christians who fail to walk in victory are really revealing that they have a messed-up belief system. God sees you in Christ. This truth, by the way, is one of the most crucial ideas for you to grasp! The more you come to understand what it means to be in Christ, the more you will come to experience your spiritual freedom.

For example, you may see yourself as a weak and struggling Christian who just can't seem to get it together. But God sees you as His dear child, holy and blameless, with everything you need to walk in victory instead of failure! Who's right?

God is! You see, deep down inside, the real you is in Christ! You are forgiven, free from sin's power, united to the One who has all power! Your failure to live in victory is due in part to the fact that you have not seen yourself as God sees you. Let God open your eyes!

When you come to a command in the Bible, the proper response is to obey it. And when Scripture states something that is true, the proper response is to believe it. It's a simple concept, but people often get it twisted by trying to do something God only expects them, by faith, to believe and accept as truth. (See Figure 11.)

Nowhere is this more likely to occur than in Romans 6:1-11. Many Christians read this section and ask, "How do I do that?" But Romans 6:1-11 is not something you can do; it's only something you can believe. And believing is the critical first step to finding the way of escape from sexual bondage.

In the Bible When You Find a:

Promise	Claim It!
Command	Obey It!
Truth	Believe It!

Figure 11—Believe It or Not!

You Are Dead to Sin

"What shall we say, then? Shall we go on sinning so that grace may increase? By no means! We died to sin; how can we live in it any longer?" (Romans 6:1,2). The defeated Christian asks, "How do I do that? How do I die to sin, especially the sexual sins which have me trapped?" The answer is, "You can't do it!" Why not? Because you have already died to sin at salvation. "We died to sin" is past tense; it has already been done.

"I can't be dead to sin," you may say, "because I don't feel dead to sin." You will have to set your feelings aside for a few verses, because it's what you believe that sets you free, not what you feel. God's Word is true whether you choose to believe it or not. Believing the Word of God doesn't make it true; His Word is true, therefore you must believe it even if your emotions don't cooperate.

"Don't you know that all of us who were baptized into Christ Jesus were baptized into his death?" (Romans 6:3). You may still be wondering, "How do I do that?" The answer is the same: You can't do it, because you have already been baptized into Christ

Jesus. It happened the moment you placed your faith in Jesus Christ as Savior and Lord. It is no good trying to seek something that the Bible tells us we already have: "We were all baptized by one Spirit into one body" (1 Corinthians 12:13). "We were" is past tense. It's done, so it must be believed.

You Have New Life

> We were therefore buried with him through baptism into death in order that, just as Christ was raised from the dead through the glory of the Father, we too may live a new life. If we have been united with him like this in his death, we will certainly also be united with him in his resurrection (Romans 6:4,5).

Have we been united with Him? Absolutely! "If we have been united with him" can literally read: "If we have become united with Him in the likeness of His death—and we certainly have—we shall also be united with him in the likeness of His resurrection."

You cannot identify with the death and burial of Christ without also identifying with His resurrection and ascension. You will live in defeat if you believe only half the gospel. You have died with Christ, and you have been raised with Him and seated in the heavenlies (Ephesians 2:6). From this position you have the authority and power to live the Christian life.

Every child of God is spiritually alive and therefore "in Christ." Paul clearly identifies every believer, young or old, as with Christ:

- in His death (Romans 6:3,6; Galatians 2:20; Colossians 3:1-3).
- in His burial (Romans 6:4).
- in His resurrection (Romans 6:5,8,11).
- in His ascension (Ephesians 2:6).
- in His life (Romans 5:10,11).
- in His power (Ephesians 1:19,20).
- in His inheritance (Romans 8:16,17; Ephesians 1:11,12).

Jesus didn't come only to die for our sins; He also came that we might have life (John 10:10). We celebrate His death on Good Friday, but we celebrate His resurrection on Easter. It is the resurrected life of Christ that God has given to us. Paul develops this truth in Romans 5:8-11: "God demonstrates his own love for us in this: While we were still sinners, Christ died for us" (verse 8). God loves you! But is that all? "Since we have now been justified by his blood, how much more shall we be saved from God's wrath through him!" (verse 9).

Isn't that great? You're not going to hell! But is that all? "For if, when we were God's enemies, we were reconciled to him through the death of his Son, how much more, having been reconciled, shall we be saved through his life!" (verse 10).

Eternal life isn't just something you get when you die. You are alive in Christ right now. But is that all? "Not only is this so, but we also rejoice in God through our Lord Jesus Christ, through whom we have now received reconciliation [peace]" (verse 11). This peaceful union assures us that our souls are in union with God, which is what it means to be spiritually alive.

Are you beginning to see hope for overcoming sexual struggles? You should, because you have already died to it and been raised to new and victorious life in Christ.

The Old You Is Gone

"For we know that our old self was crucified with him so that the body of sin might be rendered power-less, that we should no longer be slaves to sin" (Romans 6:6). The verse does not say "we do" but "we know." Your old self was crucified when Christ was crucified. Many young people are desperately trying to put to death the old self with all its tendencies to sin, but they can't do it because it is already dead! You cannot do what God alone can and has already done.

Christians who continually fail in their Christian walk begin to question incorrectly, "What experience must I have in order to live victoriously?" There is none. The only experience necessary for the above verse to be true occurred nearly 2000 years ago on the cross. And the only way we can enter into that experience today is by faith. We can't save ourselves, and we can't by human effort overcome the penalty of death or the power of sin. Only God can do that, and He has already done it.

We don't live obediently hoping that God may someday accept us. We are already accepted by God, so we live obediently. Remember—it is not what we do that determines who we are; it is who we are and what we believe that determines what we do.

Jesus went to the cross with all the sins of the world upon Him. But when He was resurrected, all of those sins stayed in the grave. He sits at the right hand of the Father today, having triumphed over sin and death. And since you are in Him, you are also dead to sin.

Many teenagers accept the truth that Christ died for the sins they have already committed. But what about the sins they commit in the future? When Christ died for all your sins, how many were then future? All of them, of course! This is not a license to sin, but a marvelous truth on which to stand against Satan's accusations. It is something we must know in order to live free in Christ.

Is Sin Gone?

Has sin disappeared then because we have died to it? Has the power of sin diminished? No, it's still strong and still appealing. But now when sin makes its appeal, we have the power to say no because our relationship with sin ended when the Lord "rescued us from the dominion of darkness and brought us into the kingdom of the Son he loves" (Colossians 1:13). Paul explains how this is possible in Romans 8:1,2: "Therefore, there is now no condemnation for those who are in Christ Jesus, because through Christ Jesus the law of the Spirit of life set me free from the law of sin and death."

Is the law of sin and death still operating? Yes, because it is a law. But a greater law has overcome it—the law of the Spirit of life. It's like flying. Can you fly by your own power? No, because the law of gravity keeps you bound to earth. But you can fly if you buy an airline ticket and apply a law greater than gravity: jet propulsion. As long as you stay in that airplane and operate according to the greater law, you will soar. But if you cease to operate under that law by stepping out the door in mid-flight, the law of gravity will quickly take effect and down you will go!

Like gravity, the law of sin and death is still here, still operative, still powerful, and still making its appeal. But you don't need to submit to it. The law of the Spirit of life is a greater law. As long as you live by the Spirit, you will not carry out the desires of the sinful nature (Galatians 5:16). You must "be strong in the Lord and in his mighty power" (Ephesians 6:10). The moment you think you can stand on your own, the moment you stop depending on the Lord, you are headed for a fall (Proverbs 16:18).

All temptation is the devil's attempt to get us to live our lives independently of God.

> So, if you think you are standing firm, be careful that you don't fall! No temptation has seized you except what is common to man. And God is faithful; he will not let you be tempted beyond what you can bear. But when you are tempted, he will also provide a way out so that you can stand up under it (1 Corinthians 10:12,13).

When we give in to temptation and are deceived by the father of lies, we should quickly repent of our sin, renounce the lies, return to our loving Father, who cleanses us, and resume the walk of faith.

Perhaps you are struggling against sexual sin, vainly trying to figure out what you must do to get free. Hopefully, the truth of Romans 6:1-11 has blown away the prison doors in your understanding. It's not what you do that sets you free; it's what you believe. God has done everything He can do through the death and resurrection of Jesus Christ. Your vital first step to freedom is to consider it so, affirm it, and stand on it.

Where the Battle Is Being Fought

But what if we have allowed sin to reign in our mortal bodies? Wouldn't we be in some form of bondage? Paul clearly describes this struggle and its solution in Romans 7:15-25. The discussion which follows is based on many counseling sessions I (Neil) have had with Christians struggling with temptation, sin, and sexuality. You may find yourself identifying with Dan as I talk through Romans 7:15-25 (NASB) with him. I trust you will also identify with the liberating truth of God's Word.[2]

Dan: Neil, I can't keep going on like this. I have been sexually active in the past, and I'm really sorry about it. I have confessed it to the Lord, but I can't seem to get victory. I don't want to live like this! It's ruining my life.

Neil: Dan, let's look at a passage of Scripture that seems to describe what you are experiencing. Romans 7:15 reads: "That which I am doing, I do not understand; for I am not practicing what I would like to do, but I am doing the very thing I hate." Would you say that pretty well describes your life?

Dan: Exactly! I really want to do what God says is right, and I hate being in bondage to this lust.

Neil: It sounds like you would identify with verse 16 as well: "But if I do the very thing I do not wish to

do, I agree with the law, confessing that it is good."
Dan, how many persons are mentioned in this verse?

Dan: There is only one person, and it is clearly "I."

Neil: It's defeating when we know what we want to
do but for some reason can't do it. How have you tried
to resolve this conflict in your own mind?

Dan: Sometimes I wonder if I'm even a Christian. It
seems to work for others, but not for me. I sometimes question if the Christian life is possible or if God is really here.

Neil: You're not alone, Dan. Many young Christians
believe they are different from others, and most think
they're the only ones who struggle with sexual temptations. If you were the only player in this battle, it would
stand to reason that you would question your salvation
or the existence of God. But look at verse 17: "So now,
no longer am I the one doing it, but sin which indwells
me." Now how many players are there?

Dan: Apparently two, "I" and "sin." But I don't
understand.

Neil: Let's read verse 18 and see if we can make
some sense out of it: "I know that nothing good dwells
in me, that is, in my flesh; for the wishing is present in
me, but the doing of the good is not."

Dan: I learned that verse a long time ago. It's easy
for me to accept that I'm no good for myself and no
good for my family. Sometimes I think it would be better if I just wasn't here.

Neil: That's not true, because that's not what the verse says. In fact it says the opposite. The "nothing good" that is dwelling in you is not you. It's something else. If I had a wood splinter in my finger it would be "nothing good" dwelling in me. But the "nothing good" is not even my flesh, but it dwells in my flesh. If we see only ourselves in this struggle, living righteously will seem hopeless. These passages tell us there is a second party involved in our struggle whose nature is evil and different from ours.

You see, Dan, when you and I were born, we were born under the penalty of sin. And we know that Satan and his demons are always working to keep us under that penalty. When God saved us, Satan lost that battle, but he didn't curl up his tail or pull in his fangs. He is now committed to keeping us under the power of sin. But in Christ we have died to sin and are no longer under its power.

We have the authority in Christ to overcome the penalty and power of sin despite Satan's lies that we are still under them. The passage we are looking at also says that this evil is going to work through the flesh, which remained with us after our salvation. It is our responsibility to crucify the flesh and to resist the devil.

Let's continue in the passage to see if we can learn more about how the battle is being waged. Verses 19-21 state: "For the good that I wish, I do not do; but I practice the very evil that I do not wish. But if I am doing the very thing I do not wish, I am no longer the one doing it, but sin which dwells in me. I find then the principle that evil is present in me, the one who wishes to do good."

Dan: Sure, it is clearly evil and sin. But isn't it just my own sin? When I sin, I feel guilty.

Neil: There's no question that you and I sin, but we are not "sin" as such. Evil is present in us, but we are not evil per se. This does not excuse us from sinning, because Paul wrote in Romans 6:12 that we are responsible not to let sin reign in our mortal bodies. When you came under conviction about your sexual sin, what did you do?

Dan: I confessed it to God.

Neil: Dan, confession literally means to agree with God. It is the same thing as walking in the light or living in moral agreement with Him about our present condition. We must confess our sin if we want to live in harmony with our Heavenly Father, but that doesn't go far enough. Confession is only the first step to repentance. The man Paul is writing about agrees with God that what he is doing is wrong, but it didn't resolve his problem. You have confessed your sin to God, but you are still in bondage to lust. It has to be frustrating for you. Have you ever felt so defeated that you just want to lash out at someone or yourself?

Dan: Almost every day!

Neil: But when you cool down, do you again have thoughts that are in line with who you really are as a child of God?

Dan: Always, and then I feel terrible about lashing out.

Neil: Verse 22 explains why: "For I joyfully concur with the law of God in the inner man." When we act out of character with who we really are, the Holy Spirit immediately brings conviction because of our union with God. Out of frustration and failure we think or say things like, "I'm not going back to church anymore. Christianity doesn't work. It was God who made me this way, and now I feel condemned all the time. God promised to provide a way of escape. Well, where is it? I haven't found it!" But soon our true nature begins to express itself. "I know what I'm doing is wrong, and I know God loves me, but I'm so frustrated by my continuing failure."

Dan: Someone told me once that this passage was talking about a non-Christian.

Neil: I know some good people who take that position, but that doesn't make sense to me. Does a natural man joyfully concur with the law of God in the inner man? Do unbelievers agree with the law of God and confess that it is good? I don't think so! In fact, they speak out rather strongly against it. Some even hate us Christians for upholding such a moral standard. Now look at verse 23, which describes the nature of this battle with sin: "But I see a different law in the members of my body, waging war against the law of my mind, and making me a prisoner of the law of sin which is in my members." According to this passage, Dan, where is the battle being fought?

Dan: The battle appears to be in the mind.

Neil: You got it! That's exactly where the battle rages. Now if Satan can get you to think you are the only one in the battle, you will get down on yourself or God when you sin, which is counterproductive to resolving the problem. Let me put it this way: Suppose you opened a door you were told not to open, and a dog came through the door and wrapped his teeth around your leg. Would you beat on yourself or would you beat on the dog?

Dan: I guess I would beat on the dog.

Neil: Of course you would. On the other side of the door, another dog—Satan—is tempting you with thoughts like, "Come on, open the door. I have an exciting video to show you. Everybody else is doing it. You'll get away with it." So you open the door and the dog comes in and grabs hold of your leg. You feel the pain of conviction and the sting of sin. Then the tempter switches to being the accuser. Your mind is pummeled with his accusations: "You opened the door. You're a miserable excuse for a Christian. God certainly can't love someone as sinful as you."

So you cry out, "God, forgive me!" And He does. But the dog is still clinging to your leg! You go through the cycle repeatedly: sin, confess, sin, confess, sin, confess. You beat on yourself continuously for your repeated failure.

People get tired of beating on themselves, so they walk away from God under a cloud of defeat and condemnation. Paul expressed this feeling in verse 24: "Wretched man that I am! Who will set me free from the body of this death?" He doesn't say he's wicked or sinful, but that he's miserable. This man is not free. His attempts to do the right thing are met in moral failure because he has submitted to God but has not resisted the devil (James 4:7). There is nobody more miserable than someone who knows what is right and wants to do what is right but can't.

Dan: That's me—miserable!

Neil: Wait a minute, Dan. There's victory. Jesus will set us free. Look at verse 25: "Thanks be to God through Jesus Christ our Lord! So then, on the one hand I myself with my mind am serving the law of God, but on the other, with my flesh the law of sin." Let's go back to the dog illustration. Why isn't crying out to God enough to solve your ongoing conflict with sexual sin?

Dan: Well, like you said, the dog is still there. I guess I have to chase off the dog.

Neil: You will also have to close the door. What have you done to resolve your sexual sins and temptations?

Dan: Like I said, I have confessed them to God and asked His forgiveness.

Neil: But as you have already found out, that didn't quite resolve the problem. Here are the steps you must take.

First, realize that you are already forgiven. Christ died once for all your sins. You were right in confessing your sin to God, because you need to own up to the fact that you opened the door when you knew it was wrong.

Second, to make sure that every door is closed, you need to ask the Lord to reveal to your mind every sexual use of your body as an instrument of unrighteousness. As the Lord brings them to your mind, renounce them. Your body belongs to God and it is not to be used for sexual immorality.

Third, present your body to God as a living sacrifice and reserve the sexual use of your body for marriage only.

Finally, resist the devil and he will flee from you.

Dan: I think I'm getting the picture. I've been condemning myself for my inability to live the Christian life. I can also see why I have been questioning my salvation. I see that Paul was frustrated about his failure, but he didn't get down on himself. He accepted his responsibility. More important, he expressed confidence by turning to God, because he knew the Lord Jesus Christ would enable him to live above sin.

Neil: You're on the right track. Condemning yourself won't help because there is no condemnation for those who are in Christ Jesus (Romans 8:1). We don't want to assist the devil in his role as the accuser. Most people who are in bondage question their salvation. I have counseled hundreds who have shared with me their doubts about God and themselves. Ironically, the very fact that they are sick about their sin and want to get out of it is one of the biggest assurances of their salvation. Non-Christians don't have those kinds of convictions.

Romans 7:15-25 contains truth you must believe about sin and Satan and implies steps of action you must take to resist him. There is one more important thing you need to know: No one particular sin, including sexual sin, is isolated from the rest of reality. To gain complete freedom, you need to walk through all the Steps to Freedom in Christ (see chapter 13). In further preparation for doing so, you also need to understand the battle which is raging for your mind. Satan is a defeated foe, but if he can get you to believe a lie, he can control your life. In the next chapter we will seek to understand how our minds function so that we can win this critical battle.

Purity Pointers

Read: Romans 6:1-11

Reflect: 1. After reading through Romans 6, what
do you believe about who you are in
Christ? In what ways is every believer
identified with Christ?

2. Because of the grace and freedom we
have in Christ should we go on sinning
so that grace may increase? Why or why
not?

3. What is temptation? Why is it so hard to
say no to something when you're in
bondage?

Respond: Dear Heavenly Father, thank You that Jesus
didn't come just to die for my sins; He also
came that I might have life (John 10:10). I
celebrate the resurrection of Jesus Christ
and my life in Him. Jesus, You are my resurrected Lord. Thank You for showing me
Your great love for me in that while I was
still a sinner You died for me. Thank You
that You didn't stop there but also justified
me and made me holy. I choose to walk in
the truth of who I am in Christ. In Jesus'
name I pray. Amen.

CHAPTER TWELVE

Choosing to Believe the Truth

Don't struggle to be better. Don't determine that you are going to try harder. Acknowledge your need of His all-sufficient grace and go forward trusting in the grace of God. "As you therefore have received Christ Jesus the Lord, so walk in Him" (Colossians 2:6 NASB). You were saved by faith; therefore you are to walk in faith. It may be one step at a time, but walk. You can say, "I can't," as long as in the next breath you say, "But God, You can."
—Kay Arthur[1]

In 1969 Doctor Sayer was battling a terrible disease in his patients called the "sleeping disease." This disease caused its victims to shake uncontrollably until finally it left them in a frozen state. Like statues they sat immovable. What was worse, their minds shut down as well. They couldn't remember the simplest detail of their own lives. They were unable to speak or even feed themselves. But one day Dr. Sayer was experimenting with a synthetic drug called El-Dopa. What happened next was incredible. Each patient given the drug experienced what Dr. Sayer called an awakening. They could speak, move freely, and remember everything. But tragically, the awakening only lasted about three months and the patients returned to their terrible frozen state.

For many young Christians trapped by sexual sin, life is filled with only a few brief awakenings. Some go to summer camp and rededicate their lives to Christ only to have their commitments fade by the time school starts. Others hear a powerful sermon and their lives are moved, but only for a short time. They soon return to their old ways of thinking and believing. Why? Because these Christians identity with the first Adam who sinned. However, those of us who have trusted Christ are no longer identified with Adam and his sin, but with Jesus and His righteousness. We are not locked outside of God's presence as Adam was. We are seated with Christ in heavenly places. The difference between Adam and Christ is eternally profound.

Our relationship with God is complete and eternal because it is provided by Christ. The Christian life is not a series of brief awakenings. When you were born spiritually, God wrote your name in Jesus' book of life (see Revelation 21:27), and you became a citizen of heaven. As long as Christ remains alive spiritually, we will remain alive spiritually—and that's forever. We must live by faith in accordance with the truth. Remember, it's not what you do that sets you free; it's what you believe.

However, according to Romans 6:12,13, there is also something we must do in response to what God has already done. But what God calls you to do in verses 12 and 13 will only be effective in your life if you believe verses 1-11. It is the truth that sets us free, and believing the truth must precede and determine responsible behavior.

Give Yourself as an Offering

Paul says, "Therefore do not let sin reign in your mortal body so that you obey its evil desires" (verse 12). So then, whose job is it not to allow sin to reign in our bodies? Clearly, it is ours. This means we cannot say, "The devil made me do it." God never commands us to do something we cannot do or that the devil can prevent us from doing. In Christ you have died to sin, and the devil can't make you do anything. He will tempt you, accuse you, and try to deceive you. But if sin reigns in your body, it is because you allow it to happen. You are responsible for your own attitudes and actions.

How then do we prevent sin from reigning in our bodies? Paul answers in verse 13: "Do not offer the parts of your body to sin, as instruments of wickedness, but rather offer yourselves to God, as those who have been brought from death to life; and offer the parts of your body to him as instruments of righteousness."

1. Don't Offer Your Body to Sin

We are not to use our eyes, hands, feet, etc. in any way that would serve sin. So when you're surfing the channel on TV and stop to watch the *Sports Illustrated* swimsuit special, letting your eyes linger lustfully on each model, you are offering your body to sin. When you try to explore someone else's body, you are offering your body to sin. When you fantasize about someone, you are offering your body to sin. Whenever you choose to offer yourself to sin, you invite sin to rule in your physical body, something God has commanded us not to do.

2. Offer Yourself and Your Body to God

Notice that Paul makes a distinction between "yourselves" and "the parts of your body." Self is who we are on the inside, the immortal part of us. Our bodies and the various parts are who we are on the outside, the mortal, temporary part of us. Someday we will be rid of these old earth suits. At that time we will be absent from our mortal bodies and present with the Lord in immortal bodies (2 Corinthians 5:8). As long as we are on planet Earth, however, our inner selves are united with our outer physical bodies. We are to offer the complete package—body, soul, and spirit—to God.

You have opportunities every day to offer your eyes, your hands, your brain, your feet, etc. to sin or to God. The Lord commands us to be good stewards of our bodies and use them only as instruments of righteousness. But ultimately it's our choice.

What happens when those of us who are united with the Lord and one spirit with Him misuse our body sexually with others? The Bible says we become one flesh with the object of our sin. Somehow we bond together. Bonding is a positive thing in a wholesome relationship. But in an immoral union, bonding only leads to bondage.

How many times have you heard of a nice Christian

girl who becomes involved with an immoral guy, has sex with him, and then continues in a sick relationship? He takes advantage of her and abuses her. Friends and relatives tell her, "He's no good for you." But she won't listen. Even though her boyfriend treats her badly, the girl won't leave him.

Why? Because a spiritual and emotional bond has formed. They have become one flesh. Such bonds must be broken. That's one reason God instructs us not to become entangled in sexual activities and relationships in the first place.

The Beauty of Offering Yourself to God

The Bible's sacrificial system provides a beautiful illustration of what it means to offer our bodies to God as instruments of righteousness instead of offering our bodies to sin.

The sin offering in the Old Testament was a blood offering. Blood was drained from the sacrificial animal, and the carcass was taken outside the camp and disposed of. Only the blood was offered to God for the forgiveness of sin. Hebrews 9:22 states, "Without the shedding of blood there is no forgiveness."

At the cross, the Lord Jesus Christ became our sin offering. After He shed His blood for us, His body was taken down and buried outside the city, but unlike the slain lamb of the Old Testament, the Lamb of God did not stay buried for long.

There was also a burnt offering in the Old Testament. Unlike the sin offering which involved only blood, the burnt offering was totally consumed on the altar—blood, carcass, everything. In the Hebrew, *burnt* literally means "that which ascends." In the burnt offering, the whole sacrificial animal ascended to God in flames and smoke from the altar. It was "an aroma pleasing to the Lord" (Leviticus 1:9).

Jesus is the sin offering, but who is the burnt offering? We are! Paul writes, "I urge you, brothers, in view of God's mercy, to offer your bodies as living sacrifices, holy and pleasing to God—which is your spiritual worship" (Romans 12:1). Our sins are forgiven; Christ did that for us when He shed His blood. But if you want to live victoriously in Christ over the sin which plagues you, you must present yourself and your body to God as an instrument of righteousness. Such a sacrifice is "pleasing to God" as was the aroma of the burnt offering in the Old Testament.

Rethink How You Think

Imagine that you have worked all though high school for the same boss, a cantankerous, unreasonable jerk. The man is known throughout the company for busting the employees, chewing them out royally for even the slightest suspicion of a mistake. You learned early on to avoid the old grouch as much as possible. Every time he walks up to you, you cringe in fear, expecting to get blasted, even if he has only come to borrow a pen.

One day you arrive at work to learn that the boss has been suddenly fired. You are no longer under his authority, and your relationship with him has ended. Your new boss is a saint—mild-mannered, kind, considerate, and affirming. He clearly has the best interests of his employees at heart. But how do you think you will behave around him? Whenever you see your new boss coming toward you, you immediately look for a place to hide, just like you did when you saw your old boss. Whenever the man comes up to you, your heart jumps into your throat—you wonder what you're going to get reamed out for this time. But the more you get to know your new boss the more you realize he is as different from your old boss as night is from day. It will take time to get to know your new boss and to change your automatic negative reaction to him because of what you experienced under the old boss.

Old habits are hard to break. Once we become programmed a certain way, it is difficult to reprogram our minds. This is especially true of established sexual thought patterns and habits which are contrary to God's Word, patterns which were possibly ingrained in us before we became Christians.

We learned from Romans 6:1-11 that we are no longer under the authority of sin and Satan. We are new creatures in Christ (2 Corinthians 5:17). But old thought patterns and habits of responding to temptation don't automatically go away. Some traumatic memories of abuse during childhood still cause us to recoil in pain. We have a new boss, Jesus Christ, but having lived under the domination of sin and Satan, we must adjust to the glorious freedom our new boss has provided for us.

How does that happen? Paul called the process renewing our minds. Having instructed us what to believe about our relationship to sin and Satan (Romans 6:1-11) and challenging us to present ourselves and our bodies to God instead of to sin (Romans 6:12,13; 12:1), Paul urges, "Do not conform any longer to the pattern of this world, but be transformed by the renewing of your mind. Then you will be able to test and approve what God's will is—his good, pleasing and perfect will" (Romans 12:2). Next to what you believe about your relationship to sin, the two most critical issues you face in overcoming sexual bondage are 1) the presentation of your physical body to God and 2) the renewing of your mind to line up with God's truth.

Why is renewing the mind so critical? Because no one can live in a way that is inconsistent with how he thinks or perceives himself. What we do doesn't determine who we are; who we are determines what we do. If you continue to think and respond as if you are under the dominion of your old boss, you will continue to live that way. You must change the way you think if you want to change your behavior.

Reprogramming the Computer

Why do we need to have our minds renewed? Let's answer that question with a brief review of our spiritual history. Because of the fall of Adam, we are all born physically alive but spiritually dead in our trespasses and sins (Ephesians 2:1). Before we placed faith in Jesus Christ, we had neither the presence of God in our lives nor the knowledge of God's ways. So we learned how to live our lives independently of God. We had no other choice.

Then one day we heard the gospel and decided to invite Jesus into our lives. We were born again. We became new creations in Christ. But unfortunately, there is no erase feature in this tremendous computer we call the mind. Everything previously programmed into our memory banks before we knew Christ is still there. Our brains have recorded every experience we have ever had, good and bad. We remember every sexual temptation and have stored away how good it felt to yield to each one. If we don't reprogram our minds we will continue to respond to temptation the way we learned to under our old boss, Satan.

The good news—literally, the gospel—gives us all the resources we need to renew our minds. The Lord has sent us the Holy Spirit, who is the Spirit of truth (John 14:16,17), and He will guide us into all truth (John 16:13). Because we are in Christ, "we have the mind of Christ" (1 Corinthians 2:16). We have superior weapons to win the battle for our minds. Paul wrote,

> For though we live in the world, we do not wage war as the world does. The weapons we fight with are not the weapons of the world. On the contrary, they have divine power to demolish strongholds. We demolish arguments and every pretension that sets itself up against the knowledge of God, and we take captive every thought to make it obedient to Christ (2 Corinthians 10:3-5)

Paul is not talking about defensive armor, but about battering-ram weaponry that tears down strongholds in our minds which have been raised up against the knowledge of God.

Practice First-Frame Thinking

If we want to take the way of escape that God has provided, we must use God's weapons and change how we respond at the first frame of every sexual temptation. For if we allow our minds to dwell on tempting thoughts, we will eventually act on them. So we must take those first thoughts captive and make them obedient to Christ.

Suppose you struggle with lust. One night your mom asks you to go to the store for milk. When you get into the car, you wonder which store you should go to. You remember that the local convenience store has a display of pornographic magazines within easy reach. You can buy milk at other stores which don't sell those magazines. But the memory of the seductive photos you have ogled before at the convenience store give rise to a tempting thought. The more you think about it, the harder it is to resist. When you pull out of the driveway, which way do you turn?

On the way to the convenience store, all kinds of thoughts cross your mind. You pray, "Lord, if You don't want me to look at the pornography, have my youth pastor be in the store buying milk or cause the store to be closed." Since the store is open (do you know any convenience stores that ever close?!) and since the youth pastor isn't there, you decide it must be okay to take a look. The mind has an incredible way of rationalizing, which is why you must stop tempting thoughts before your mind can come up with a reason to act on them.

But your stolen pleasure doesn't last. Before you leave the store, guilt and shame overwhelm you. "Why did I do it?" you moan. You did it primarily because you ignored the way of escape available to you before you even pulled out of the garage. You failed to take that initial thought captive and make it obedient to Christ.

Hardware and Software

The Bible says that we have an outer self and an inner self (2 Corinthians 4:16). We need to understand how our outer self (our physical body) relates to our inner self (our soul or spirit). Our brain is part of the outer self. Our mind is a part of the inner self. These are two very different things. Our brain is little more than meat. When we die physically our outer self, including our brain, will return to dust. Our inner self will be absent from the body. We will be brainless, but we will not be mindless.

God has obviously created the outer self to go with the inner self. The relationship between the mind and the brain is clear.

Our mind is the software. As the brain receives input from the external world through the five senses, the mind compiles, analyzes, and interprets the data and chooses responses based on how the mind has been programmed. Before we came to Christ, our minds were programmed by the world, the flesh, and the devil, and we made choices without the knowledge of God or the benefit of His presence. When we became Christians, nobody pressed the CLEAR button in our minds. We need reprogramming by God's truth. We need our minds renewed.

The Danger of Watching

One of the ways we program our mind is through the eye-gate: what we see. Powerful things can happen in just seconds when we see something.

Have you ever wondered why it is so hard to

remember some things and to forget others? You study all night for a test and then pray that the facts won't leave you before you take the big exam. But just one glance at a sexually explicit image seems to stay in the mind for years. Why is that?

When we experience feelings of excitement, including visual stimulation by sexually-charged images, an autonomic signal is sent to the adrenal glands. A hormone called epinephrine goes into the bloodstream, which locks a picture into the memory at the time of the excitement. This reaction causes us to involuntarily remember emotionally-charged events, bad or good. If you could get excited about some of your subjects in school, you would remember them better!

The Danger of Thoughts

Just as we can't control our glands, we can't control our emotions. If you think you can, try liking someone right now that you don't like! We can't order our emotions that way, and the Bible doesn't ask us to. We must recognize our emotions, because we can't be right with God if we aren't real about how we feel. But we can't tell ourselves not to feel. What we do have control over is how we think, and how we think controls how we feel. And the Bible does tell us to control our thinking: "Brothers, stop thinking like children. In regard to evil be infants, but in your thinking be adults" (1 Corinthians 14:20).

Our feelings are primarily a product of our thought life. What we believe, how we think, and how we think of ourselves and the world around us determines how we feel.

Suppose you are paddling a canoe down an awesome river in the wilderness, enjoying God's creation and a cool Dr Pepper. You round a bend in the river, and standing on the riverbank is someone of the opposite sex. From a distance the person is good looking and motions to you. A blanket is spread on the riverbank, and your mind and emotions suddenly go wild from the tempting possibilities. Your heart begins to pound and your palms grow sweaty. "What an incredible opportunity. We're all alone out here. I can get away with this." Ignoring any conviction, you paddle toward the shore, your emotions up to 9.9 on a scale of 10.

But as you draw near the shore, you see a deflated raft and an expression of distress on the person's face. It's clear that the person isn't waving you to the shore for a romantic date but needing help. You suddenly realize that your first impression of the stranger was wrong, and your emotions quickly drop to a .1.

Your feelings had responded to what you believed was the truth, but what you *felt* was a distortion of reality. Our feelings can be distorted by what we choose to think or believe. If what we choose to believe does not reflect truth, then what we feel will not reflect reality. If you want to feel right you must think right.

Choose to Think the Truth

There is someone active in the world today who doesn't want you to think or believe the truth about God, yourself, Christian maturity, or sexual purity. Paul writes, "The Spirit clearly says that in later times some will abandon the faith and follow deceiving spirits and things taught by demons" (1 Timothy 4:1). We have counseled hundreds of people who struggle with their thoughts. In every case the root problem has been a spiritual battle for their minds. No wonder Paul exhorts us, "Finally, brothers, whatever is true, whatever is noble, whatever is right, whatever is pure, whatever is lovely, whatever is admirable—if anything is excellent or praiseworthy—think about such things" (Philippians 4:8). What joy we would feel if we saw life from God's point of view and could think only His thoughts!

If Satan can get us to believe a lie, he can control our lives. He is intent on destroying our view of God, ourselves, members of the opposite sex, and the world we live in. Our current problems don't only come from what we believed in the past. Paul says we are to presently and continuously take every thought captive and make it obedient to Christ (2 Corinthians 10:5).

One way Satan gains access to us is through our unwillingness to forgive those who have hurt us. If you were ever sexually abused and now struggle with thoughts like, "I can't forgive that person," "I hate that person," or "I don't want to forgive him. I want him to suffer as much as he made me suffer," Satan has outwitted you. He knows that your bitterness will keep you trapped by your past. You must now renounce those schemes and choose to believe and forgive from your heart all those who have hurt you.

Look at 2 Corinthians 4:4: "The god of this age has blinded the minds of unbelievers, so that they cannot see the light of the gospel of the glory of Christ." The one who raises up thoughts against the knowledge of God has a field day with the sexually abused. "Where is your God now?" he taunts. "If God is love, why does He allow the innocent to suffer? If God is all powerful, why didn't He stop that person from violating you?" Such is the smoke screen of lies Satan uses to blind us to the truth. Paul said, "I am afraid that just as Eve was deceived by the serpent's cunning, your minds may somehow be led astray from your sincere and pure devotion to Christ" (2 Corinthians 11:3).

Satan is the father of lies and the one who leads our minds astray. He works on our minds to destroy our concept of God and our understanding of who we are as children of God. Satan can't do anything about our position in Christ, but if he can get us to believe we don't really have one, we will live that out, even though it's a lie.

Satan preys on the minds of wounded teenagers—the victim of a broken home, the child of an alcoholic, someone who was sexually abused as a child, and others. They are prime candidates for Satan's lies because their minds have already been pummeled with self-doubt, fear, anger, and hatred because of their circumstances. But you don't have to be the victim of a broken home or a painful childhood to be the target of the enemy's sexual temptations, accusations, and deceptions.

For example, suppose in a vulnerable moment a young girl has a tempting sexual thought toward someone of the same sex. She can't believe she could be tempted with homosexuality. She is embarrassed and immediately flees from the tempting situation. She tells no one about it. Who would understand? But then it happens again. And again. And she begins to wonder, "Why am I thinking like this? Could I be one of them?" Once the door of doubt is open, she seriously questions her sexuality.

If she continues to dwell on those tempting thoughts, it will affect the way she feels. That's the way God made us—our feelings are based on how we think. But if she believes what she feels and behaves accordingly, she will use her body as an instrument of unrighteousness. Sin will then reign in her mortal body. Unless she takes those thoughts captive and makes them obedient to Christ, she is on her way to sexual bondage.

Don't assume that all disturbing thoughts are from Satan. We live in a sinful world with tempting images and messages all around us. You have memories of hurtful experiences which prompt thoughts contrary to the knowledge of God. But whether these thoughts are introduced into your mind from your memory bank, the television set, the pit itself, or your own imagination doesn't matter much, because the answer to this is always the same: Choose to reject the lie and think the truth.

You can work hard to figure out the source of every thought, but it won't solve the problem. Someone may be able to give you a brilliant answer as to what's wrong and still not know the solution. The answer is Christ. His truth will set us free.

Cleaning Up the Mind

Can we change the way we think—even if we're trapped by pornography, fantasy, or other sexual behaviors? Yes! We can reprogram our minds. Will this take time? Yes, we will spend the rest of our lives renewing our minds and developing our character. We will never be perfect in our understanding on this earth, nor will our character be perfect like Christ's, but this is what we go after.

Christian growth can only take place when we are free in Christ. When people aren't free in Christ they go from book to book, from youth pastor to youth pastor, and from counselor to counselor, but nothing seems to work. Watch how fast they can grow, however, when they are free in Christ!

Think of a polluted mind as a 44-oz. cup filled to the top with Coke. Sitting beside the Coke is a huge bowl of crystal-clear ice, which represents the Word of God. Your goal is to purify the contents in the cup by adding ice cubes to it. Every cube displaces some of the Coke and dilutes the rest, making it a little purer. You can only put in one or two cubes a day, so the process seems futile at first. But over the course of time the water begins to look less and less polluted, and the taste and smell of Coke becomes weaker. The process continues to work—provided you don't add more Coke to the cup.

Paul writes, "Let the peace of Christ rule in your hearts, since as members of one body you were called to peace. And be thankful" (Colossians 3:15). How do we rid ourselves of evil thoughts, purify our mind, and allow the peace of Christ to reign?

We find the answer in Colossians 3:16: "Let the word of Christ dwell in you richly." Also, "How can a young man keep his way pure? By living according to your word. I seek you with all my heart; do not let me stray from your commands. I have hidden your word in my heart that I might not sin against you" (Psalm 119:9-11). Just trying to stop thinking bad thoughts won't work. We must fill our minds with the crystal-clear Word of God. This is God's plan for us.

Winning the battle for your mind may initially be a two-steps-forward, one-step-back process as you take on the world, the flesh, and the devil. But gradually it will become three steps forward, one step back, then four and five steps forward as you learn to take every thought captive and make it obedient to Christ. You may despair with all your steps backward, but God won't give up on you.

Freedom to be all that God has called you to be is the greatest blessing in this present life. This freedom is worth fighting for. As you learn more about who you are as a child of God and about the nature of the battle waging for your mind, the process gets easier. Eventually it will be 20 steps forward and one back, and finally your steps will all be forward ones, with only an occasional slip in the battle for the mind.

Purity Pointers

Read: Colossians 3:15,16; Psalm 119:9-11

Reflect: 1. Why does God ask us to give our body as an offering to God? Jesus became the sin offering. What offering did we become?

2. Why do we need our minds renewed? Can we control our glands and emotions? Can we control our thoughts?

3. What happens if you fail to take an initial sinful thought captive and make it obedient to Christ?

4. What role does God's Word play in reprogramming our minds?

Respond: Dear Heavenly Father, I want to know the truth that will set me free in Christ. Lord, I don't want to be deceived. Please reveal to me any way that I'm being tricked by the enemy. Lord, I choose to think on whatever is true, whatever is noble, whatever is right, whatever is pure, whatever is lovely, whatever is admirable and the things that are praiseworthy (Philippians 4:8). In Jesus' name I pray. Amen.

> *They will come to their senses and escape*
> *from the trap of the devil, who has taken*
> *them captive to do his will.*
> *II Timothy 2:26*

──Chapter Thirteen──

Steps to Freedom in Christ

A broken world will never be rebuilt until we learn the principle of an unbound heart. It must be unwrapped and exposed to the light. The light will show some unattractive evil, but something wonderful will happen. The love of God will be free to flood into the dark recesses, and rebuilding will begin. The Bible calls this unbinding process REPENTANCE.
—Gordon McDonald[1]

Perhaps your lack of peace and victory regarding the sexual sin in your life has worn you down. Try as you might to fight it, you keep falling into the same thoughts and behaviors again and again. You're too tired to run away anymore. You're ready to take the way of escape Christ has provided for you.

As we have indicated throughout this book, a key part to finding your freedom is taking the specific Steps to Freedom in Christ. In this chapter we will take you through those steps.

Spiritual freedom is meant for every Christian, young or old. But what does it mean to be "free in Christ"? It is to have the desire and power to worship God and do His will. It is to know God's truth, believe God's truth, and live according to God's truth. Being free in Christ means release from the chains of the sins of our past, problems of the present, and fears of the future. It is to walk with God in the power of the Holy Spirit and to experience a life of love, joy, and peace. It is not a life of perfection, but progress! All these qualities may not be yours now, but they are meant for everyone who is in Christ.

If you have received Christ as your Savior, He has already set you free through His victory over sin and death on the cross. But if freedom is not a constant reality for you, it may be because you do not understand how Christ can help you deal with the pain of your past or the problems of your present life. It is your responsibility as one who knows Christ to do whatever is needed to maintain a right relationship with God. Your eternal life is not at stake; you are safe and secure in Christ. But you will not experience all that Christ has for you if you fail to understand who you are in Christ and fail to live according to that truth.

We've got great news for you! You may be young but you are not a helpless victim caught between two nearly equal but opposite heavenly superpowers, God and Satan. Only God is all-powerful, always present, and all-knowing. Sometimes, however, the presence and power of sin and evil in our lives can seem more real to us than the presence and power of God. But that is part of Satan's tricky lie. Satan is a deceiver, and he wants you to think he is stronger than he really is. But he is also a defeated enemy, and you are in Christ, the Victor. Understanding who God is and who you are in Christ are the two most important factors in determining your daily victory over sin and Satan. False beliefs about God, not understanding who you are as a child of God, and making Satan out to be as powerful and present as God are the greatest causes of spiritual defeat.

The battle is for your mind. You may experience nagging thoughts like, "This isn't going to work," or "God doesn't love me." These thoughts are lies, implanted in your mind by deceiving spirits. If you believe them, you will really struggle as you work through these steps. These opposing thoughts can control you only if you believe them.

If you are working through these steps by yourself, don't pay attention to any lying or threatening thoughts in your mind. If you're working through the steps with a trusted friend, youth pastor, parent, or counselor (which we strongly recommend), then share any opposing thoughts with that person. Whenever you uncover a lie and choose to believe the truth, the power of Satan is broken.

As believers in Christ, we can pray with authority to stop any interference by Satan. Here is a prayer and declaration to get you started. Read them (and all prayers and declarations in these steps) out loud

Prayer

Dear Heavenly Father, we know that You are always here and present in our lives. You are the only all-knowing, all-powerful, ever-present God. We desperately need You, because without Jesus we can do nothing. We believe the Bible because it tells us what is really true. We refuse to believe the lies of Satan. We stand in the truth that all authority in heaven and on earth has been given to the resurrected Christ. Because we are in Christ, we share His authority in order to make followers of Jesus and set captives free. We ask You to protect our thoughts and minds and lead us into all truth. We choose to submit to the Holy Spirit. Please reveal to our minds everything You want to deal with today. We ask for and trust in Your wisdom. We pray for Your complete protection over us. In Jesus' name. Amen.

Declaration

In the name and the authority of the Lord Jesus Christ, we command Satan and all evil spirits to let go of (name) in order that (name) can be free to know and choose to do the will of God. As children of God, seated with Christ in the heavenlies, we agree that every enemy of the Lord Jesus Christ be bound and gagged to silence. We say to Satan and all of his evil workers that you cannot inflict any pain or in any way stop or hinder God's will from being done today in (name) life.

Following are seven steps that can free you from your past. You will cover the areas where Satan most often takes advantage of us and where strongholds have been built. Christ purchased your victory when He shed His blood for you on the cross. You will experience your freedom when you make the choice to believe, confess, forgive, renounce, and forsake. No one can do that for you. The battle for your mind can only be won as you personally choose truth.

As you go through these Steps to Freedom in Christ, remember that Satan cannot read your mind, thus he won't obey your thoughts. Only God knows what you are thinking. As you go through each step, it is important that you submit to God inwardly and resist the devil by reading each prayer out loud—verbally renouncing, forgiving, confessing, etc.

You are going to take a thorough look at your life in order to get radically right with God. It may turn out that you have another kind of problem (not covered in these steps) which is negatively affecting your life. But if you are open and honest during this time, you will greatly benefit by becoming right with God and close to Him again.

May the Lord greatly touch your life during this time. He will give you the strength to make it through. It is essential that you work through all seven steps, so don't allow yourself to become discouraged and give up. Remember, the freedom that Christ purchased for all believers on the cross is meant for *you!*

Step 1: Counterfeit Versus Real

The first step toward experiencing your freedom in Christ is to renounce (to reject and turn your back on all past, present, and future involvement with) any participation in Satan-inspired occult practices, things done in secret, and non-Christian religions. You must renounce any activity and group which denies Jesus Christ, offers direction through any source other than the absolute authority of the written Word of God, or requires secret initiations, ceremonies, promises, or pacts (covenants). Begin with the following prayer:

> Dear Heavenly Father, I ask You to reveal to me anything that I have done or that someone has done to me that is spiritually wrong. Reveal to my mind any and all involvement I have knowingly or unknowingly had with cult or occult practices, and/or false teachers. I want to experience Your freedom and do only Your will. I ask this in Jesus' name. Amen.

Even if you took part in something as a game or as a joke, you need to renounce it. Satan will try to take advantage of anything he can in our lives. Even if you just stood by and watched others do it, you need to renounce it. Even if you did it just once and had no idea it was evil, still you need to renounce it. You want to remove any and every possible foothold of Satan in your life.

Non-Christian Spiritual Checklist

(Please check all those that apply to you)

- ❑ Out-of-body experience (astral projection)
- ❑ Ouija board
- ❑ Bloody Mary
- ❑ Light as a feather (or other occult games)
- ❑ Magic Eight Ball
- ❑ Mormonism (Latter-Day Saints)
- ❑ Jehovah Witness
- ❑ New Age
- ❑ New Age medicine
- ❑ Masons
- ❑ Christian Science

- ❏ Table lifting or body lifting
- ❏ Using spells or curses
- ❏ Attempting to control others by putting thoughts in their heads
- ❏ Automatic writing
- ❏ Spirit guides
- ❏ Fortune telling
- ❏ Tarot cards
- ❏ Palm reading
- ❏ Astrology/Horoscopes
- ❏ Hypnosis
- ❏ Black or white magic
- ❏ Dungeons & Dragons (or other fantasy role-playing games)
- ❏ Video or computer games involving occult powers or cruel violence
- ❏ Blood pacts or cutting yourself on purpose
- ❏ Objects of worship/ crystals/good luck charms
- ❏ Sexual spirits
- ❏ Martial Arts (involving Eastern mysticism meditation or devotion to sensei)
- ❏ Buddhism (including Zen)
- ❏ Rosicrucianism
- ❏ Hinduism

- ❏ Science of the Mind
- ❏ Science of Creative Intelligence
- ❏ The Way International
- ❏ Unification Church (Moonies)
- ❏ The Forum (EST)
- ❏ Church of the Living Word
- ❏ Children of God (Children of Love)
- ❏ Seances
- ❏ Scientology
- ❏ Unitarianism

- ❏ Roy Masters
- ❏ Silva Mind Control

- ❏ Transcendental Meditation (TM)
- ❏ Yoga
- ❏ Hare Krishna

- ❏ Bahaism
- ❏ Native American spirit worship

- ❏ Idols of rock stars, actors/actresses, sports heroes, etc.
- ❏ Islam
- ❏ Black Muslim

(NOTE: This is not a complete list. If you have any doubts about an activity not included here, renounce your involvement in it. If it has come to mind here, trust that the Lord wants you to renounce it.)

ANTI-CHRISTIAN MOVIES

_____

_____

_____

ANTI-CHRISTIAN MUSIC

_____

_____

_____

ANTI-CHRISTIAN TV SHOWS OR VIDEO GAMES

_____

_____

_____

_____

_____

ANTI-CHRISTIAN BOOKS, MAGAZINES, AND COMICS

_____

_____

_____

_____

_____

1. Have you ever heard or seen or felt a spiritual being in your room?

2. Have you had an imaginary friend that talked to you?

3. Have you ever heard voices in your head or had repeating negative, nagging thoughts such as "I'm dumb," "I'm ugly," "Nobody loves me," "I can't do anything right," etc. as if a conversation were going on in your head? Explain.

4. Have you or anyone in your family ever consulted a medium, spiritist, or channeler? If yes, who?

5. What other spiritual experiences have you had that would be considered out of the ordinary (telepathy, speaking in a trance, known something supernaturally, contact with aliens, etc.)?

6. Have you ever been involved in satanic worship of any kind or attended a concert at which Satan was the focus?

7. Have you ever made a vow or pact?

Once you have completed the above checklist, confess and renounce each item you were involved in by praying aloud the following prayer (repeat the prayer separately for each item on your list):

> Lord, I confess that I have participated in
> _____. I thank You for Your forgiveness
> and I renounce any and all influence and
> involvement with _____.

If you have been involved in any satanic rituals or heavy occult activity (or you suspect it because of blocked memories, severe and recurring nightmares, or sexual bondage), you need to say out loud the following special renunciations and affirmations.

Read across the page, renouncing the first item in the column under "Domain of Darkness" and then affirming the first truth in the column under "Kingdom of Light." Continue down the entire list in that manner.

Domain of Darkness

Kingdom of Light

1. I renounce ever signing my name over to Satan or having my name signed over to Satan by someone else.

1. I announce that my name is now written in the Lamb's Book of Life.

2. I renounce any ceremony where I was wed to Satan.

2. I announce that I am the Bride of Christ.

3. I renounce any and all covenants, agreements, or promises that I made with Satan.

3. I announce that I have made a new covenant with Jesus Christ alone.

4. I renounce all satanic assignments for my life, including duties, marriage, and children.

4. I announce and commit myself to know and do only the will of God and I accept only His guidance for my life.

5. I renounce all spirit guides assigned to me.

5. I announce and accept only the leading of the Holy Spirit.

6. I renounce ever giving of my blood in the service of Satan.

6. I trust only in the shed blood of my Lord Jesus Christ.

7. I renounce ever eating flesh or drinking blood in satanic worship.

7. By faith I eat only the flesh and drink only the blood of the Lord Lord Jesus in Holy Communion.

8. I renounce all guardians and satanic parents that were assigned to me.

8. I announce that God is my Heavenly Father and the Holy Spirit is my guardian by whom I am sealed.

9. I renounce any baptism whereby I am identified with Satan.

9. I announce my baptism into Christ Jesus and my identity is now in Him.

10. I renounce every sacrifice made on my behalf by which Satan may claim ownership of me.

10. I announce that only the sacrifice of Christ has any claim on me. I belong to Him. I have been purchased by the blood of the Lamb.

Step 2: Deception Versus Truth

God's Word is true, and we need to accept the truth deep in our hearts (Psalm 51:6). When King David lived a lie, he really suffered. When he finally found freedom by admitting that he'd sinned, he wrote, "Blessed is the man . . . in whose spirit is no deceit" (Psalm 32:2). We must stop lying to ourselves and to each other and speak the truth in love (Ephesians 4:15,25). Mentally healthy young people can face the truth, live in a real world, and not let fear control them. Scripture tells us that God is the only one we should fear. This means that we hold Him in highest respect and are in great awe of His power, majesty, and holiness.

Start this important step by praying the following prayer out loud. Don't let opposing thoughts such as "This isn't going to work," "This is a waste of time," or

"I wish I could believe this but I just can't" keep you from praying and choosing the truth. Belief is a choice. If you choose to believe what you feel, then Satan, the "father of lies," will keep you in bondage. We must choose to believe what God says, regardless of what our feelings tell us. Even if it's difficult for you, pray the following prayer.

> Dear Heavenly Father, I know that You want me to face the truth and that I must be honest with You. I know that choosing to believe the truth will set me free. I have been deceived by Satan, the father of lies, and I have deceived myself as well. I thought I could hide from You, but You see everything and still love me. I pray in the name of the Lord Jesus Christ, asking You to rebuke all of Satan's demons through Him, who shed His blood and rose from the dead for me.
>
> I have trusted in Jesus alone to save me, and so I am Your child. Therefore, by the authority of the Lord Jesus Christ, I command all evil spirits to leave my presence. I ask the Holy Spirit to lead me into all truth. I ask You, Father, to look deep inside me and know my heart. Show me if there is anything in me that I am trying to hide, because I want to be free. In Jesus' name. Amen.

Take some time now to let God reveal any of Satan's evil tricks that he's used against you in your life. False teachers and deceiving spirits can fool you, but you can also fool yourself. Now that you are alive in Christ and forgiven, you don't need to live a lie or defend yourself like you used to. Christ is now your truth and defense.

Ways You Can Deceive Yourself

❑ Hearing God's Word but not doing it (James 1:22; 4:17)
❑ Saying I have no sin (I John 1:8)
❑ Thinking I am something I'm not (Galatians 6:3)
❑ Thinking I am wise in the things of the world
  (1 Corinthians 3:18, 19)
❑ Thinking I will not reap what I sow (Galatians 6:7)
❑ Thinking that ungodly people who live lives of sin
  will share in God's kingdom (1 Corinthians 6:9)
❑ Thinking I can hang out with bad people and they
  won't have any influence on me (1 Corinthians 15:33)
❑ Thinking I can be a good Christian and still hurt
  others by what I say (James 1:22)

Use the following prayer of confession for each item
above that you have believed. Pray through each item
separately.

> Lord, I confess that I have deceived myself
> by _____ . I thank You for Your forgive-
> ness and commit myself to believing Your truth.

Wrong Ways of Defending Yourself

❑ Refusing to face the bad things that have happened
  to me (denial of reality)
❑ Escaping from the real world by daydreaming, TV,
  movies, computer or video games, music, etc. (fantasy)
❑ Withdrawing from people to avoid rejection
  (emotional isolation)
❑ Reverting (going back) to a less-threatening time of
  life (regression)

❑ Taking out frustrations on others (displaced anger)
❑ Blaming others for my problems (projection)
❑ Making excuses for poor behavior (rationalization)

Use the following prayer of confession for each item above that you have participated in. Pray through each item separately.

> Lord, I confess that I have defended myself wrongly by _____. I thank You for Your forgiveness and commit myself to trusting in You to defend and protect me.

Choosing the truth may be difficult if you have lived a lie and have been deceived for some time. The Christian needs only one defense, Jesus. Knowing that you are completely forgiven and accepted as God's child sets you free to face reality and declare your total dependence upon Him.

Faith is the biblical response to the truth, and believing the truth is a choice we can all make. If you say, "I want to believe God, but I just can't" you are being deceived. Of course you can believe God because what God says is always true.

Faith is something you decide to do, whether or not you feel like doing it. Believing the truth doesn't make it true, however. *It's true; therefore we believe it.*

Simply "having faith" is not the key issue here. It's what or who you believe in that makes the difference. Everybody believes in something and everybody lives according to what he or she believes. The question is: Is the object of your faith trustworthy? If what you believe is not true, then how you live will not be right.

Read aloud the following Statement of Truth, thinking

about the words as you read them. Read it every day for several weeks. This will help you renew your mind and replace any lies you have believed with the truth

Statement of Truth

1. I believe there is only one true and living God (Exodus 20:2,3) who is the Father, Son, and Holy Spirit. He is worthy of all honor, praise, and glory. I believe He made all things and holds all things together (Colossians 1:16,17).

2. I recognize Jesus Christ as the Messiah, the Word who became flesh and lived with us (John 1:1,14). I believe He came to destroy the works of the devil (1 John 3:8).

3. I believe that God showed His love for me by having Jesus die for me, even though I was sinful (Romans 5:8). I believe that God rescued me from the dark power of Satan and brought me into the kingdom of His Son, who forgives my sins and sets me free (Colossians 1:13,14).

4. I believe I am spiritually strong because Jesus is my strength. I have authority to stand against Satan because I am God's child (1 John 3:1-3). I believe I was saved by the grace of God through faith, that it was a gift and not the result of any works of mine (Ephesians 2:8,9).

5. I choose to be strong in the Lord and in the strength of His might (Ephesians 6:10). I put no confidence in the flesh (Philippians 3:3) because my

weapons of spiritual battle are not of the flesh but are powerful through God for the tearing down of Satan's strongholds (2 Corinthians 10:4). I put on the whole armor of God (Ephesians 6:10-20), and I resolve to stand firm in my faith and resist the evil one (I Peter 5:8,9).

6. I believe that apart from Christ I can do nothing (John 15:5), yet I can do all things through Him who strengthens me (Philippians 4:13). Therefore, I choose to rely totally on Christ. I choose to abide in Christ in order to bear much fruit and glorify the Lord (John 15:8). I announce to Satan that Jesus is my Lord (1 Corinthians 12:3), and I reject any counterfeit gifts or works of Satan in my life.

7. I believe that the truth will set me free (John 8:32). I stand against Satan's lies by taking every thought captive in obedience to Christ (2 Corinthians 10:5). I believe that the Bible is the only reliable guide for my life (2 Timothy 3:15,16). I choose to speak the truth in love (Ephesians 4:15).

8. I choose to present my body as an instrument of righteousness, a living and holy sacrifice, and to renew my mind with God's Word (Romans 6:13; 12:1,2). I put off the old self with its evil practices and put on the new self (Colossians 3:9,10). I am a new creation in Christ (2 Corinthians 5:17).

9. I ask my Heavenly Father to direct my life and to give me power to live by the Holy Spirit (Ephesians 5:18), so that He can guide me into all truth (John 16:13). He will give me strength to live above sin and not carry out the desires of my flesh. I crucify the flesh, choose to

be led by the Holy Spirit and to obey Him (Galatians 5:16,24).

10. I renounce all selfish goals and choose the greatest goal of love (I Timothy 1:5). I choose to obey the two greatest commandments to love the Lord my God with all my heart, soul, and mind, and to love my neighbor as myself (Matthew 22:37-39).

11. I believe that Jesus has all authority in heaven and on earth (Matthew 28:18) and that He rules over everything (Colossians 2:10). I believe that Satan and his demons have been defeated by Christ and are subject to me since I am a member of Christ's body (Ephesians 1:19,20; 2:6). So, I obey the command to submit to God and to resist the devil (James 4:7) and I command Satan, by the authority of the Lord Jesus Christ, to leave my presence.

Step 3: Bitterness Versus Forgiveness

When you fail to forgive those who hurt you, you become a wide-open target for Satan. God commands us to forgive others as we have been forgiven (Ephesians 4:32). You need to obey this command so that Satan can't take advantage of you (2 Corinthians 2:11). Christians are to forgive others and show them mercy because our Heavenly Father has shown mercy to us. Ask God to bring to your mind the names of those people you need to forgive by praying the following prayer out loud. (Remember to let this prayer come from your heart as well as your mouth!)

Dear Heavenly Father, I thank You for Your great kindness and patience which has led me to turn from my sins (Romans 2:4). I know I have not been completely kind, patient, and loving toward those who have hurt me. I have had bad thoughts and feelings toward them. I ask You to bring to my mind all the people I need to forgive (Matthew 18:35). I ask You to bring to the surface all my painful memories so that I can choose to forgive these people from my heart. I pray this in the precious name of Jesus who has forgiven me and who will heal me from my hurts. Amen.

On a sheet of paper, make a list of the people who come to your mind. At this point, don't question whether you need to forgive a certain person or not. If a name comes to your mind, write it down.

Finally, write "me" at the bottom of the list. Forgiving yourself means accepting God's cleansing and forgiveness. Also, write "thoughts against God." We sometimes harbor angry thoughts toward God.

We can expect or even demand that He act in a certain way in our lives, and when He doesn't do what we want in the way we want, we can get angry. Those feelings can become a wall between us and God, and even though we don't actually need to forgive Him because He is perfect, we do need to let the feelings go.

Before you begin working through the process of forgiving the people on your list, stop and consider what real forgiveness is and what it is not.

Forgiveness is not forgetting. People who would like to forget all their pain before they get around to forgiving someone, usually find they cannot. God commands us to forgive now. Confusion sometimes arises about this because Scripture says that God will remember our

sins no more (Hebrews 10:17). But God knows everything and can't "forget" as if He had no memory of our
sin. God promises to never use your past against you
(Psalm 103:10). And so, you may not be able to forget
your past, but you can be free from it by forgiving others. When we bring up the past and use it against others, we are showing that we have not yet forgiven them
(Mark 11:25).

Forgiveness is a choice, a decision of the will. Since God
requires us to forgive, it is something we can do.
Forgiveness seems hard because it pulls against our
sense of what is right and fair. We naturally want
revenge for the things we have suffered. But we are told
by God never to take our own revenge (Romans 12:19).

You might be thinking, "Why should I let them off
the hook?" And that is exactly the problem. As long as
you do not forgive, you are still hooked to those who
hurt you. You are still chained to your past. *By forgiving,
you let them off your hook, but they are not off God's hook.*
We must trust Him to deal with the other person justly,
fairly, and mercifully, something we cannot do.

You say, "But you don't know how much this person hurt me." But until you let go of your hate and
anger, they will continue to be able to hurt you. You
finally stop the pain by forgiving them. You forgive for
your sake, so that you can be free. *Forgiveness is mainly
an issue of obedience between you and God.* God wants you
to be free; this is the only way.

*Forgiveness is agreeing to live with the consequences of
another person's sin.* Forgiveness costs you something.
You choose to pay the price for the evil you forgive. But
you will live with the consequences whether you want to
or not. Your only choice is whether you will do so in the
bondage of bitterness or in the freedom of forgiveness.

Of course, Jesus took the eternal consequences of all sin upon Himself. God "made him who had no sin to be sin for us, so that in him we might become the righteousness of God" (2 Corinthians 5:21). We need, however, to accept the temporary consequences of what was done to us. But no one truly forgives without suffering the pain of another's sin. That can seem unfair and we wonder, where is the justice? It is found at the cross which makes forgiveness legally and morally right. As those who crucified Jesus mocked and jeered, Jesus prayed, "Father, forgive them for they do not know what they are doing" (Luke 23:34).

How do you forgive from your heart? You allow God to bring to the surface the mental agony, emotional pain, and feelings of hurt toward those who hurt you. If your forgiveness doesn't reach down to the emotional core of your life, it will be incomplete. Too often we try to bury the pain inside us, making it hard to get in touch with how we really feel. Though we may not know how to or even want to bring our feelings to the surface, God does. Let God bring the pain to the surface so that He can deal with it. This is where God's gentle healing process begins.

Forgiveness is the decision not to use that offense against them. It is not unusual for us to remember a past, hurtful event and find the anger and hate we felt returning. It is tempting to bring up the issue with the one who hurt us in order to make them feel bad. But we must choose to take that thought of revenge captive to the obedience of Christ, and choose to maintain forgiveness.

This doesn't mean you must continue to put up with the future sins of others. God does not tolerate sin and neither should you. Nor should you put yourself in the position of being continually abused and hurt by the sins of others. You need to take a stand against sin while continuing to forgive those who hurt you.

Don't wait to forgive until you feel like forgiving. You will never get there. Your emotions will begin to heal, once you have obeyed God's command to forgive. Satan will have lost his power over you in that area and God's healing touch will take over. For now, it is freedom that will be gained, not necessarily a feeling.

As you pray, God may bring to mind painful memories you had totally forgotten. Let Him do this, even if it hurts. God wants to free you; forgiving these people is the only way. Don't try to excuse the offender's behavior, even if it is someone close to you.

Remember, forgiveness is dealing with your own pain and leaving the other person to deal with God. Good feelings will follow in time. Freeing yourself from the past is the critical issue right now.

Don't say, "Lord, please help me to forgive." He is already helping you and will be with you all the way through the process. Don't say, "Lord, I want to forgive" because that bypasses the hard choice we have to make. Say, "Lord, I forgive." As you move down your list, stay with each individual until you are sure you have dealt with all the remembered pain, everything the person did that hurt you, and how it made you feel (rejected, unloved, unworthy, dirty, etc.).

It's time to begin. For each person on your list, pray aloud:

> Lord, I forgive (name the person) for (what they did to hurt you) even though it made me feel (the painful memories or feelings).

Once you have dealt with every offense that has come to your mind and you have honestly expressed how that person hurt you, then conclude by praying:

> Lord, I choose not to hold any of these things against (name) any longer. I thank You for setting me free from the bondage of my bitterness toward (name). I choose now to ask You to bless (name). In Jesus' name. Amen.

Step 4: Rebellion Versus Submission

We live in rebellious times. Often young people today don't respect people that God has placed in positions of authority over them. You may have a problem living in submission to authority. You can easily be deceived into thinking that those in authority over you are robbing you of your freedom. In reality, however, God has placed them there for your protection.

Rebelling against God and His authorities is serious business. It gives Satan an opportunity to attack you. Submission is the only solution. God requires more of you, however, than just the outward appearance of submission. He wants you to sincerely submit to your authorities, especially parents, from the heart. When you submit, your commanding general, the Lord Jesus Christ, is telling you to "Get into ranks and follow Me!" He promises that He will not lead you into temptation, but will deliver you from the evil one (Matthew 6:13).

The Bible makes it clear that we have two main responsibilities toward those in authority over us: to pray for them and submit to them. Pray the following prayer out loud from your heart.

Dear Heavenly Father, You have said in the Bible that rebellion is the same thing as witchcraft, and being self-willed is like serving false gods (1 Samuel 15:23). I know that I have disobeyed and rebelled in my heart against You and those You have placed in authority over me. I thank You for Your forgiveness for my rebellion. I pray that You will show me all the ways I have been rebellious. I choose to adopt a submissive spirit and servant's heart. In Jesus' precious name I pray. Amen.

Placing ourselves under authority is an act of faith! By submitting, we are trusting God to work through His lines of authority.

At times parents, teachers, and other authority figures may abuse their authority and break the laws which are ordained by God for the protection of innocent people. In those cases, you need to seek help from a higher authority for your protection. The laws in your state may require you to report such abuse to the police or other protective agencies.

If there is continuing abuse (physical, mental, emotional, or sexual) at home, counseling may be needed to change this situation.

If authorities abuse their position by asking you to break God's law or compromise your commitment to Him, you need to obey God rather than man (Acts 4:19,20).

We are all told to submit to one another out of reverence for Christ (Ephesians 5:21). In addition, however, God uses specific lines of authority to protect us and give order to our daily lives.

❏ Civil government (including traffic laws, drinking laws, etc.) (Romans 13:1-7; 1 Timothy 2:1-4; 1 Peter 2:13-17)

❏ Parents, stepparents, or legal guardians (Ephesians 6:1-3)

❏ Teachers, coaches, and school officials (Romans 13:1-4)

❏ Your boss (Romans 13:1-4)

❏ Husband (Ephesians 5:22-24)

❏ Church leaders (pastor, youth pastor, Sunday school teacher) (Hebrews 13:17)

❏ God Himself (Daniel 9:5,9)

Examine each of the seven areas of authority listed above and ask the Lord to forgive you for those times you have not respected these positions or submitted to them, by praying:

> Lord, I agree with You that I have been rebellious toward _____. Please forgive me for this rebellion. I choose to be submissive and obedient to Your Word. In Jesus' name. Amen.

Step 5: Pride Versus Humility

Pride is a killer. Pride says, "I can do it! I can get myself out of this mess without God or anyone else's help." Oh no we can't! We absolutely need God, and we desperately need each other. Paul wrote, "We . . . worship by the Spirit of God . . . glory in Christ Jesus, and . . . put no confidence in the flesh" (Philippians 3:3).

Humility is confidence properly placed in God. We are to be "strong in the Lord and in the strength of His might" (Ephesians 6:10). James 4:6-10 and 1 Peter 5:1-10 tell us that spiritual problems will follow when we are proud. Use the following prayer to express your commitment to live humbly before God.

Dear Heavenly Father, You have said that pride goes before destruction and a haughty spirit before a fall (Proverbs 16:18). I confess that I have been thinking mainly of myself and not of others. I have not denied myself, picked up my cross daily, and followed You (Matthew 16:24), and as a result, I have given ground to the enemy in my life. I have believed that I could be successful by living according to my own power and resources. I now confess that I have sinned against You by placing my will before Yours and by centering my life around myself instead of You. I renounce my pride and my selfishness and close any doors I've opened in my life or my physical body to the enemies of the Lord Jesus Christ. I choose to rely on the Holy Spirit's power and guidance so that I can do Your will. I give my heart to You and stand against all of Satan's attacks. I ask You to show me how to live for others. I now choose to make others more important than myself and to make You the most important of all in my life (Romans 12:10; Matthew 6:33). Please show me specifically now the ways in which I have lived pridefully. I ask this in the name of my Lord Jesus Christ. Amen.

Having made that commitment in prayer, now allow God to show you any specific areas of your life where you have been prideful, such as:

❑ I have a stronger desire to do my will than to do God's will.

❑ I rely on my own strengths and abilities rather than on God's.

❑ I too often think my ideas are better than other people's ideas.

❑ I want to control how others act rather than develop self-control.

❑ I sometimes consider myself more important than others.

❑ I have a tendency to think I don't need other people.

❑ I find it difficult to admit when I am wrong.

❑ I am more likely to be a people-pleaser than a God-pleaser.

❑ I am overly concerned about getting credit for doing good things.

❑ I often think I am more humble than others.

❑ I often think I am smarter than my parents.

❑ I often feel my needs are more important than others' needs.

❑ I consider myself better than others because of my academic, artistic, or athletic abilities and accomplishments.

For each of the above areas that have been true in your life, pray out loud:

> Lord, I agree I have been prideful in the area of _____ . Thank You for forgiving me for this pridefulness. I choose to humble myself and place all my confidence in You. Amen.

Step 6: Bondage Versus Freedom

The next step to freedom deals with the sins that have become habits in your life. If you have been caught in the vicious cycle of "sin-confess-sin-confess," realize that the road to victory is "sin-confess-*resist*" (James 4:7). Habitual sin often requires help from a trusted brother or sister in Christ. James 5:16 says, "Confess your sins to each other and pray for each other so that you may be healed. The effective prayer of a righteous man is powerful and effective." Seek out a stronger Christian who will lift you up in prayer and hold you accountable in your areas of weakness.

Sometimes the assurance of 1 John 1:9 is sufficient: "If

we confess our sins, He is faithful and just and will forgive us our sins and purify us from all unrighteousness."

Remember, confession is not saying, "I'm sorry"; it's openly admitting, "I did it." Whether you need the help of others or just the accountability of God, pray the following prayer out loud:

> Dear Heavenly Father, You have told us to put on the Lord Jesus Christ and make no provision for the flesh in regard to its lust (Romans 13:14 NASB). I agree that I have given in to sinful desires which wage war against my soul (1 Peter 2:11). I thank You that in Christ my sins are forgiven, but I have broken Your holy law and given the devil an opportunity to wage war in my body (Romans 6:12,13; James 4:1; 1 Peter 5:8). I come before Your presence now to admit these sins and to seek Your cleansing (1 John 1:9) that I may be freed from the bondage of sin. I now ask You to reveal to my mind the ways that I have broken Your moral law and grieved the Holy Spirit. In Jesus' precious name I pray. Amen.

There are many habitual sins that can control us. The following list contains some of the more common sins of the flesh. Look through the list and ask the Holy Spirit to reveal to your mind which ones you need to confess. He may bring to mind others that are not here. For each one God reveals, pray the following prayer of confession from your heart.

❑ stealing   ❑ perfectionism
❑ lying   ❑ cheating

- ❑ fighting
- ❑ hatred
- ❑ jealousy, envy
- ❑ anger
- ❑ complaining and criticism
- ❑ impure thoughts
- ❑ swearing

- ❑ gossiping
- ❑ procrastination
- ❑ greed/materialism
- ❑ apathy/laziness
- ❑ eagerness for lustful pleasure
- ❑ other

> Lord, I admit that I have committed the sin of _____. I thank You for Your forgiveness and cleansing. I turn away from this sin and turn to You, Lord. Strengthen me by Your Holy Spirit to obey You. In Jesus' name. Amen.

It is our responsibility to take control over sin in our bodies. We must not use our bodies or someone else's as an instrument of unrighteousness (Romans 6:12,13). If you are struggling with sexual sins you can't stop (such as pornography, masturbation, heavy petting, heavy kissing, oral sex, or sexual intercourse) pray as follows:

> Lord, I ask You to reveal to my mind every sexual use of my body as an instrument of unrighteousness. In Jesus' precious name I pray. Amen.

As the Lord brings to your mind every sexual use of your body, whether it was done to you (i.e., rape, incest, or any sexual molestation) or willingly by you, renounce every occasion:

> Lord, I renounce (name the specific use of your body) with (name the person involved)

and I ask You to break that sinful bond with (name).

After you have completed this exercise, commit your body to the Lord by praying out loud from your heart:

> Lord, I renounce all these uses of my body as an instrument of unrighteousness, and I admit my willful participation. Lord, I choose to present my eyes, my mouth, my mind, my hands and feet, my whole body to You as instruments of righteousness. I now present my body to You as a living sacrifice, holy and acceptable unto You, and I choose to reserve the sexual use of my body (my sexual organs) for marriage only (Hebrews 13:4).
>
> I reject the lie of Satan that my body is not clean or that it is dirty or in any way unacceptable to You as a result of my past sexual experiences. Lord, I thank You that You have totally cleansed and forgiven me, and that You love me just as I am. Therefore, I can accept myself and my body as cleansed in Your eyes. In Jesus' name. Amen.

Special Prayers for Specific Needs

Homosexual

> Lord, I renounce the lie that You have created me or anyone else to be homosexual, and I agree that You clearly forbid homosexual behavior. I accept myself as a child of God and declare that You created me a man (or a

woman). I renounce all homosexual thoughts, urges, or drives, as well as any bondage of Satan, that have perverted my relationships with others. I announce that I am free to relate to the opposite sex and my own sex in the way that You intended. In Jesus' name. Amen.

Abortion

Lord, I confess that I was not a proper guardian and keeper of the life You entrusted to me, and I ask Your forgiveness. I choose to accept Your forgiveness by forgiving myself, and I now commit that child to You for Your care for all eternity. In Jesus' name. Amen.

Suicidal Tendencies

I renounce suicidal thoughts and any attempts I may have made to take my own life or in any way injure myself. I renounce the lie that life is hopeless and that I can find peace and freedom by taking my own life. Satan is a thief, and he comes to steal, kill, and destroy. I choose life in Christ who said He came to give me life and give it to the full. I choose to accept Your forgiveness by forgiving myself, and I choose to believe that there is always hope in Christ. In Jesus' name. Amen.

Eating Disorders or Cutting on Yourself

I renounce the lie that my value as a person is dependent upon my physical beauty, my weight or size. I renounce cutting myself, vomiting, using laxatives, or starving myself as a means of cleansing myself of evil or altering my appearance. I announce that only the blood of the Lord Jesus Christ cleanses me from sin. I accept the reality that there may be sin present in me due to the lies I have believed and the wrongful use of my body. But I renounce the lie that I am evil or that any part of my body is evil. My body is the temple of the Holy Spirit and I belong to God. I am totally accepted by God in Christ, just as I am. In Jesus' name. Amen.

Substance Abuse

Lord, I confess that I have misused substances (alcohol, tobacco, food, prescription or street drugs) for the purpose of pleasure, to escape reality, or to cope with difficult problems. I confess that I have abused my body and programmed my mind in a harmful way. I have not allowed Your Holy Spirit to guide me. I ask Your forgiveness, and I reject any satanic connection or influence in my life because of my misuse of drugs or food. I cast my cares onto Christ who loves me, and I commit myself to no longer give in to substance abuse, but instead allow the Holy Spirit to lead and empower me. In Jesus' name. Amen.

After you have confessed all known sin, pray:

I now confess these sins to You and claim,

through the blood of the Lord Jesus Christ, my forgiveness and cleansing. I cancel all ground that evil spirits have gained through my willful involvement in sin. I ask this in the wonderful name of my Lord and Savior Jesus Christ. Amen.

Step 7: Curses Versus Blessings

The last step to freedom is to renounce the sins of your ancestors and any curses which may have been placed on you. In giving the Ten Commandments, God said, "You shall not make for yourself an idol, in the form of anything in heaven above or on the earth beneath or in the waters below. You shall not bow down to them or worship them; for I, the Lord your God, am a jealous God, punishing the children for the sin of the fathers to the third and fourth generation of those who hate me" (Exodus 20:4,5).

Demonic or familiar spirits can be passed on from one generation to the next, if you don't renounce the sins of your ancestors and claim your new spiritual heritage in Christ. *You are not guilty for the sin of your ancestors,* but because of their sin, Satan has gained access to your family.

In addition, deceived and evil people may try to curse you, or satanic groups may try to target you. You have all the authority and protection you need in Christ to stand against such curses. In order to walk free from the sins of your ancestors and any demonic influences, read the following declaration and pray the following prayer out loud. Let the words come from your heart as you remember the authority you have in Christ Jesus.

Declaration

I here and now reject and disown all the sins of my ancestors. As one delivered from the domain of darkness into the kingdom of God's Son, I cancel out all demonic working that was passed down to me from my family. As one who is crucified and raised with Jesus Christ and who sits with Him in heavenly places, I renounce all satanic assignments that are directed toward me. I cancel out every curse that Satan and his workers have put on me. I announce to Satan and all his forces that Christ became a curse for me (Galatians 3:13) when He died for my sins on the cross. I reject any and every way in which Satan may claim ownership of me. I belong to the Lord Jesus Christ who purchased me with His own blood. I reject all the blood sacrifices whereby Satan may claim ownership of me. I declare myself to be eternally and completely signed over and committed to the Lord Jesus Christ. By the authority that I have in Jesus Christ, I now command every familiar spirit and every enemy of the Lord Jesus Christ that is influencing me to leave my presence. I commit myself to my Heavenly Father, to do His will from this day forward.

Prayer

Dear Heavenly Father, I come to You as Your child, purchased by the blood of the Lord Jesus Christ. You are the Lord of the universe and the Lord of my life. I submit my body to You as an instrument of righteousness, a living sacrifice, that I may glorify You in my body. I now ask Your Holy Spirit to lead and empower me to know and do Your will. I commit myself to the renewing of my mind in order to prove that Your will is good, perfect, and acceptable for me. All this I do in the name and authority of the Lord Jesus Christ. Amen.

Purity Pointers

Read: Galatians 5:1

Reflect: 1. Which of the Steps to Freedom seemed to help you most? Is there anything you still need to deal with?

2. Why is it the person of Christ who brings freedom and not these steps?

3. If you find yourself in bondage again can these truths help you?

4. In what way could you share this message of hope and freedom with other teens? Do you think they would listen?

Respond: Dear Heavenly Father, You said that the truth would set me free and You were right. Thank You for showing me the road to freedom in Christ. I ask You now to help me grow, as I choose to maintain my freedom. Jesus, You are the Bondage Breaker. Thank You for never giving up on me and always loving me. In Jesus' name I pray. Amen.

> *It is for freedom that Christ has set us free.*
> *Stand firm, then, and do not let yourselves*
> *be burdened again by a yoke of slavery.*
> *Galatians 5:1*

---CHAPTER FOURTEEN---

Living Free and Staying Free

When we think of holiness, great saints of the past like Francis of Assisi or George Mueller spring to mind—but holiness is not the private thing just for an elite corps of martyrs. Holiness is the everyday business of every Christian. It shows itself in the decisions we make and the things we do, hour by hour, day by day.

—Charles Colson[1]

Your experience of moving through the Steps to Freedom in Christ and being set free from bondages may be different from anyone else's. Why? Because each individual is unique, and each has his or her own unique set of issues to resolve. Some people are happy because of the overwhelming sense of peace they feel for the very first time. Others may have to work through many layers yet to come. God is gracious and doesn't hurry us through everything at once, especially if the process is a difficult one. Getting free and staying free in Christ are two different issues.

Staying Free

Paul wrote, "It is for freedom that Christ has set us free" (Galatians 5:1). Once we have tasted freedom in Christ, how do we keep it? We continue to stand in the truth of who we are in Christ. Paul completes the verse by encouraging, "Stand firm, then, and do not let yourselves be burdened again by the yoke of slavery." We must be careful that we don't turn our freedom in Christ into rules and regulations (legalism) or use it as an opportunity to go on sinning (license) (Galatians 5:13).

The steps you took to find your freedom were not the end of a journey but the beginning of a walk in the Spirit. Paul teaches us, "Live by the Spirit, and you will not gratify the desires of the old nature" (Galatians 5:16). You worked through the Steps to Freedom in chapter 13 and gained your freedom: Now you must maintain it. You have won an important battle, but the war goes on. So now we'll look at six Bible-based guidelines that will help you maintain your freedom and walk in Christ.

Remember that you don't become holier or get on God's good side if you follow these six guidelines. Neither do you lose your holiness if you ignore them. God loves you whether you follow His guidelines or not. However, His desire is that you choose to follow His guidelines and walk in the freedom He won for you through the sacrificial death of His Son, your Savior, Jesus Christ.

1. Strengthen Your Freedom with Fellowship

"For you know that it was not with perishable things such as silver or gold that you were redeemed from the empty way of life handed down to you from your forefathers, but with the precious blood of Christ, a lamb without blemish or defect" (1 Peter 1:18,19).

By now you know that God has completely accepted you in Christ, but you might be wondering what happens to your relationship with God when you sin. Doesn't sin block His acceptance of you? No way! God's acceptance is a relationship issue not a fellowship issue.

When I (Dave) watched my first child come into the world, my wife and I decided to give him my name, first and last. Not only does little Dave have my name but he also has my blood flowing through his veins, even the same type O negative. Is there anything little Dave could possibly do which would change his blood relationship with me, his father? What if he ran away from home and changed his name? What if he disowned me? Would he still be my son? Of course! We're related by blood and nothing can change that.

But is there anything he could do which would affect how we get along together as father and son? Yes! Whenever little Dave disobeys me, the harmony of our fellowship is interrupted. But our relationship never is. He's always my son, and I always love and accept him.

When you sin you don't destroy your relationship with God, because you're related to Him through the blood of Christ. Your fellowship with Him will suffer when you disobey His will, but you have been born again into His family. You're forever His child. He will always love and accept you. When you sin you don't

need to re-accept Christ. You simply need to get your
fellowship back in order by asking God to forgive you
and then renouncing the way you behaved (1 John 1:9).

So where should you place your effort in the process
of spiritual growth and maturity? Not in your relationship to God, because there's nothing you can do to
improve upon it other than to continue to believe it is
true. You are a child of God. You can't become any more
of a child of God than what your spiritual birth made
you, so stop trying. Rather, make time for fellowship
with your Father, determine that you'll believe what He
says is true, and then obey Him. The result will be spiritual growth and a peace with God as you fellowship
with Him.

Staying free also means developing positive relationships with others. God never intended that we live
the Christian life alone. That's why He created the
church. We need God, but we also desperately need the
loving fellowship of the body of Christ.

In Hebrews 10:25 God reminds us, "Let us not give
up meeting together, as some are in the habit of doing,
but let us encourage one another—and all the more as
you see the Day approaching." And Hebrews 3:13 "But
encourage one another daily, as long as it is called
Today, so that none of you may be hardened by sin's
deceitfulness." So, what are believers called to do?

There are different kinds of relationships, and we
need each of them. Open up to your family. No other
humans know you better than do the members of your
family. Give them access to your heart through honest
communication. This makes your relationship vulnerable to growth and brings about healthy intimacy. In our
homes and churches, we must speak the truth in love
(Ephesians 4:25) and walk in the light (1 John 1:6-8).

Trouble is a possibility in all human relationships, but if we seek the truth, trouble will be minimized and usually solvable.

Another important relationship for you to cultivate is one with a spiritually mature believer of your gender—a big brother or big sister in the faith. Ask this person to disciple you and spur you on in your Christian life. A mature Christian can be your spiritual reference point, helping you maintain your walk in the Lord, providing accountability and modeling for your walk of faith. Ask God to direct you to the individual whom He has chosen to fill this role at this time in your life.

Get involved in a youth group that has leaders who understand freedom in Christ and your journey. Together you can help pace each other and encourage forward motion in your daily walk. Maturity is not instantaneous but a gradual progression.

What happens when we worship, pray, and study God's Word together? We strengthen our belief systems. But being together does more than that. Your godly friends can help you manage your emotions. Your emotions may lead you away from what God is calling you to believe, and friends can help you see the truth. What happens to you and your walk of faith at these times? You grow up! Friendships with brothers and sisters in the Lord are a big key to your successful walk of faith.

2. Strengthen Your Freedom by Studying God's Word

If you will read God's Word, you will come to know God. Reading His Word, studying it, and memorizing key verses will help strengthen your freedom in Christ. How is your Bible study and your quiet time coming along?

What could you do to be more faithful?

What is the best time for you to read and study the Bible?

What place is best for you?

What format is best for you?

Who can you go to for guidance and direction?

What is a step you can take to improve your Bible study time?

In 2 Timothy 2:15, you are instructed to "be diligent to present yourself approved to God as a workman who does not need to be ashamed, handling accurately the word of truth" (NASB). No one can do this for you.

3. Strengthen Your Freedom Through Daily Prayer

Proverbs 15:8 tells us that God "delights in the prayers of his people" (TLB). And because of the relationship with God which Christ's death on the cross made possible, we are free to go before God on our own whenever we want to.

Commit yourself to daily prayer. Prayer is dependence upon God. You can pray these suggested prayers often and with confidence:

Daily Prayer

Dear Heavenly Father, I honor You as my Lord. I know that You are always present with me. You are the only all-powerful and only wise God. You are kind and loving in all Your ways. I love You and I thank You that I am united with Christ and spiritually alive in Him. I choose not to love the world, and I crucify the flesh and all its passions.

I thank You for the life that I now have in Christ, and I ask You to fill me and guide me with Your Holy Spirit so that I may live my life free from sin. I declare my dependence upon You, and I take my stand against Satan and all his lying ways. I choose to believe the truth, and I refuse to be discouraged. You are the God of all hope, and I am confident that You will meet my needs as I seek to live according to Your Word. I express with confidence that I can live a responsible life through Christ who strengthens me.

I now take my stand against Satan and command him and all his evil spirits to depart from me. I put on the whole armor of God. I submit my body as a living sacrifice and renew my mind by the living Word of God in order that I may prove that the will of God is good, acceptable, and perfect. I ask these things in the powerful and precious name of my Lord and Savior Jesus Christ. Amen.

Bedtime Prayer

Thank You, Lord, that You have brought me into Your family and have blessed me with every spiritual blessing in the heavenly realms in Christ. Thank You, too, for providing this time of renewal through sleep. I accept it as part of Your perfect plan for Your children, and I trust You to guard my mind and my body during sleep. As I have thought about You and Your truth during the day, I choose to let those thoughts continue in my mind while I am asleep. I commit myself to You for Your protection from every attempt of Satan or his demons to attack me during the night. I commit myself to You as my rock, my fortress, and my resting place. I pray in the strong name of the Lord Jesus Christ. Amen.

4. Strengthen Your Freedom by Taking Every Thought Captive

If you want to stay free in Christ, you must assume responsibility for your thought life. Taking every thought captive to the obedience of Christ (2 Corinthians 10:5), you must reject the lies, choose the truth, and stand firm in your position in Christ.

Continue to seek your identity and sense of worth through who you are in Christ. Renew your mind with the truth that your acceptance, security, and significance is in Christ alone. Meditate on the following truths daily, reading the entire list out loud, morning and evening, over the next few weeks.

Who Am I?

Because I am in Christ . . .

I am like salt for everyone on earth (Matthew 5:13).
I am like light for the whole world (Matthew 5:14).
I am a child of God (John 1:12).
I am part of the true vine, joined to Christ and able to produce lots of fruit (John 15:1,5).
I am Christ's chosen friend (John 15:15).
I am chosen by Christ to bear fruit (John 15:16).
I am Christ's personal witness sent out to tell everybody about Jesus (Acts 1:8).

I am a slave of righteousness who pleases God (Romans 6:18).

I am enslaved to God; this makes me holy and gives me eternal life (Romans 6:22).

I am a son of God; I can call Him my Father (Romans 8:14,15; Galatians 3:26; 4:6).

I am promised an inheritance and will share in Christ's glory (Romans 8:17).

I am a temple of the Holy Spirit. His Spirit and His life live in me (1 Corinthians 3:16; 6:19).

I am united to the Lord and am one spirit with Him (1 Corinthians 3:16; 6:19).

I am a part of Christ's Body and a member of His family (1 Corinthians 12:27).

I am a new person; my past is forgiven and everything is new (2 Corinthians 5:17).

I am at peace with God, and He has given me the work of making peace between Himself and others (2 Corinthians 5:18,19).

I am a son of God through faith in Christ (Galatians 3:26,28).

I am God's child and will be given the inheritance He has promised (Galatians 4:6,7).

I am a saint, a holy one (Ephesians 1:1; Philippians 1:1, Colossians 1:2).

I am God's building project—His handiwork—born anew in Christ to do His work (Ephesians 2:10).

I am a citizen of heaven with the rest of God's family (Ephesians 2:19).

I am a prisoner of Christ, so I can help others (Ephesians 3:1; 4:1).

I am righteous and holy (Ephesians 4:24).

I am a citizen of heaven seated in heaven right now (Philippians 3:20; Ephesians 2:6).

I am hidden with Christ in God (Colossians 3:3).

I am an expression of the life of Christ because He is my life (Colossians 3:4).

I am chosen of God, holy and dearly loved, one of His special people (Colossians 3:12; 1 Thessalonians 1:4).

I am a son of the light and belong to the light and not to darkness (1 Thessalonians 5:5).

I am chosen to share in God's heavenly calling (Hebrews 3:1).

I am part of Christ; I share in His life (Hebrews 3:14).

I am one of God's living stones, being built up in Christ as a spiritual house (1 Peter 2:5).

I am a member of a chosen race, a royal priesthood, a holy nation, a people for God's own possession (1 Peter 2:9).

I am an alien and a stranger to this world in which I temporarily live (1 Peter 2:11).

I am an enemy of the devil (1 Peter 5:8).

I am a child of God, and I will be like Christ when He returns (1 John 3:1,2).

I am born of God, and the evil one cannot touch me (1 John 5:18).

I am not the great "I am" (Exodus 3:14; John 8:24,28,58), but by the grace of God, I am what I am (1 Corinthians 15:10).

Since I am in Christ, by the Grace of God . . .

I am justified through faith—I have peace with God (Romans 5:1).

I am no longer a slave to sin; the person I used to be died with Christ and now sin has no rule over my life (Romans 6:1-6).

I am free from all condemnation (punishment) that my sin has brought on me (Romans 8:1).

I have been placed into Christ by God's doing (1 Corinthians 1:30).

I have been given God's Spirit so that I can recognize the blessings God has given me (1 Corinthians 2:12).

I have the mind of Christ; I can understand what He is thinking (1 Corinthians 2:16).

I was bought at a price; I am not my own; I belong to God (1 Corinthians 6:19,20).

I am God's possession, secure in Him (sealed) because I have been given the Holy Spirit as a promise guaranteeing that I will receive all that God has stored up for His people (2 Corinthians 1:21; Ephesians 1:13,14).

Since I have died, I no longer live for myself, but for Christ (2 Corinthians 5:14,15).

I have been made righteous (acceptable) to God (2 Corinthians 5:21).

I have been crucified with Christ and it is no longer I who live, but Christ lives in me. The life I am now living is Christ's life (Galatians 2:20).

I am blessed with every spiritual blessing (Ephesians 1:3).

I was chosen in Christ before the world was created to be holy and I am without blame before Him (Ephesians 1:4).

I was predestined (chosen) by God—to be adopted as God's child (Ephesians 1:5).

I am alive with Christ; I have been given His awesome grace (Ephesians 2:5).

I am raised up and seated with Christ in heaven (Ephesians 2:6).

I have direct access to God through the Spirit (Ephesians 2:18).

I may approach God with courage, freedom, and confidence (Ephesians 3:12).

I have been rescued from the dark power of Satan's rule and have been brought into the kingdom of Christ (Colossians 1:13).

I am forgiven of all my sins and set free. The debt against me is canceled (Colossians 1:14).

Christ Himself lives in me (Colossians 1:27).

I am firmly rooted in Christ and am now being built up in Him (Colossians 2:7).

I have been made fully grown (complete) in Christ (Colossians 2:10).

I have been buried, raised, and made alive with Christ (Colossians 2:12,13).

I died with Christ and I am now raised up with Christ. My life is hidden with Christ in God. Christ is now my life (Colossians 3:1-4).

I have a spirit of power, love, and self-control (2 Timothy 1:7).

I am saved and called to a holy life (2 Timothy 1:9; Titus 3:5).

I have been made holy and set apart (sanctified) into Christ's family. That's why He is not ashamed to call me His brother or sister (Hebrews 2:11).

I have the right to come bravely before the throne of God where I will receive mercy and find grace (Hebrews 4:16).

I have been given great and awesome promises so that His nature would become part of me (2 Peter 1:4).

Remember, you are trying to turn on the light, and

you do so by choosing the truth whenever a lie comes your way.

5. Strengthen Your Freedom by Understanding Who You Are in Christ

Second Corinthians 5:16,17 says, "So from now on we regard no one from a worldly point of view. Though we once regarded Christ in this way, we do so no longer. Therefore, if anyone is in Christ, he is a new creation; the old has gone, the new has come!"

His name was Lyle Alzado, and he was one of the toughest men who had ever played football. As a defensive end, he was like a heat-seeking missile. He used his strength and speed to lock onto anyone who had the football, and his guidance system usually left the other guy drilled into the ground. Two times he was made all-pro at his position, and he played for the silver-and-black Raiders.

To make the Raider team, you had to play like a crazed animal and do whatever it took to win. At one time, though, Lyle thought he would never make the team. He only weighed 195 pounds, and while that may seem impressive to us, at that size, he simply couldn't make it in the NFL. So Lyle decided to take steroids and work out like a man with a mission. Soon he was a monstrous 300-pound defensive machine.

No one can question Lyle's heart, but he did make some poor choices. His decision to take steroids brought him success and fame, but only for a short time. The drugs transformed Lyle's body into a mountain of muscle, but it is also believed that those same chemicals brought on the brain cancer that ended his life. Lyle Alzado died in 1992 at only 43 years old. His life was literally cut in half. He thought playing football would make him somebody special and bring him importance and meaning in life. What if Lyle had never played football? Would his wife and family still love him? Of course they would. His high level of football success wasn't worth dying for.

Our identity comes from our relationship with Christ. We are complete people and our lives are extremely important because of what Christ did for us. If you are looking to anything else to bring importance and meaning to your life, you're doing the same thing Lyle did. Oh, you may not play football or pop steroids, but when you look toward anything other than Christ for your identity, you're deceived. The only identity equation that works in God's kingdom is Christ + You = A complete and meaningful life.

You will grow in freedom as you continue to better understand and more fully accept your identity and worth in Christ. And you can do that by filling your mind with the truth from God's Word about the acceptance, security, and significance which is yours in Christ.

6. Strengthen Your Freedom Through Sharing Your Faith

As one of God's children, you have the privilege and responsibility of telling others how you came to know Jesus as Savior and how you came to experience your freedom in Christ. You don't need to share your sexual struggles, but you do need to share God's truth as you understand it in the Bible. It's the truth that sets you free, and it's the truth that will set your friends free.

Again, it is our hope that, through this book, you have come to know Jesus Christ better and that, through

Him, you have been set free—free to be yourself and free to grow in Christ. Know that He will always be there for you even when your purity is under pressure.

Purity Pointers

Read: 1 Peter 1:18,19; Hebrews 10:25; Ephesians 4:25; 1 John 1:6-8; Proverbs 15:8

Reflect: 1. Why might your experience of going through the Steps to Freedom in Christ and being set free be different from anyone else's? Why do some have to work through many layers?

2. Why does your freedom in Christ need to be maintained? What are the things you need to put in place to help sustain your freedom?

3. What happens when you worship, pray, and study God's Word with other believers? When your emotions don't line up with what God is calling you to believe, how does He often use your friends to help you see the truth?

4. What did you learn about yourself from the "Who Am I?" and "Since I am in Christ, by the Grace of God . . ." lists? How did you feel about yourself after reading about who you are in Christ? What do you understand more clearly as a result of reading these statements?

Respond: Dear Heavenly Father, I know that all things are possible for me if they are God's will. I know it's Your will that I walk free in Christ. So I accept my responsibility to walk free in my Christian faith. I use my authority in Christ to stand against the enemy and any way he might try to interfere with my walk of faith. I thank You that even if I stumble and sin, I know how to get right with You. Thank You for Your great love and guidance that makes my freedom possible. In Jesus' name I pray. Amen.

Notes

Chapter 1: Who You Are

1. Billy Graham, *Storm Warning* (Dallas, TX: Word Publishers, 1992), p. 42.
2. "Sex Education: A New Philosphy for America," *The Family in America* (Mount Morris, IL: The Rockford Instructive Center on Family in America, 1989), p. 3.
3. *Life* magazine.

Chapter 2: Picking Your Peers

1. Josh McDowell, *What I Wish My Parents Knew About My Sexuality* (San Bernardino, CA: Here's Life Publishers, 1987), p. 29.
2. Margery Williams, *The Velveteen Rabbit*, public domain.

Chapter 3: Dating in 3D

1. Greg Laurie, *God's Design for Christian Dating* (Eugene, OR: Harvest House Publishers, 1983), p. 13
2. Tom Watson, Jr., *Sex and the Christian Teen, 101* (Grand Rapids, MI: Baker Book House, 1989), p. 131.
3. Barry St. Clair and Bill Jones, *Dating: Picking and Being a Winner* (San Bernadino, CA: Here's Life Publishers, 1987), p. 27.
4. "Christian Society Today," a publication of the American Family Association (January 1994), p. 3.

Chapter 4: Am I Really in Love?

1. Dr. James Dobson, *Preparing for Adolescence* (Ventura, CA: Vision House, 1980), p. 91.
2. Taken from *Living Free in Christ* by Neil Anderson (Ventura, CA: Regal Books, 1993). Used by permission.
3. Portions adapted from "Is It Love or Lust?" by Dennis Rigstad. First published in *Psychology for Living* (Rosemead, CA: Narramore ChristianFoundation).

Chapter 5: God's View on Sex

1. Bill Hybels and Rob Wilkins, *Tender Love* (Chicago, IL: Moody Press, 1993), p. 15.

Chapter 6: Why God Says Wait

1. Greg Speck, *Sex: It's Worth Waiting For* (Chicago, IL: Moody Press, 1989), p. 55.
2. Adapted from *Rebuilding Your Broken World* by Gordon McDonald (Nashville, TN: Oliver Nelson Publishers, 1988), p. 150.
3. Joe McIlhaney, *Sexuality and Sexually Transmitted Diseases* (Grand Rapids, MI: Baker Book House, 1990), p. 14.
4. Gordon McDonald, *Rebuilding Your Broken World*, p. 162.

Chapter 7: Detecting the Dangers in a Sex-Crazed World

1. Tony Campolo, "Sex Ed's Failure Rate," *Christianity Today* (February 3, 1993), p. 22.
2. "In Defense of a Little Virginity," *Focus on the Family* (1992).
3. Dr. Donald P. Orr, "Premature Sexual Activities as an Indicator of Psychological Risk," *Journal of the American Academy of Pediatrics* 87 (February 1991), p. 141.

Chapter 8: Pathways to a Dead End

1. Adapted from *Sanctity of Life* by Charles Swindoll (Dallas, TX: Word Publishers, 1990), pp. 57-58.
2. C.S. Lewis, *The Lion, The Witch and The Wardrobe* (New York, NY: Macmillan Publishing Company, 1950), p. 33.
3. Maxine Hancock and Karen Burton-Mains, *Child Sexual Abuse: A Hope for Healing* (Wheaton, IL: Harold Shaw Publishers, 1987), p. 12.
4. Herant A. Katchadourian, M.D. and Donald T. Lunde, M.D., *Fundamentals of Human Sexuality*, third edition (New York: Holt, Rinehart, and Winston Publishers, 1980), p. 379.
5. Barbara Chester, *Sexual Assault and Abuse* (San Francisco: Harper and Row Publishers, 1987), pp. 23-24.

Chapter 9: The Seduction of Your Mind

1. Charles Stanley, *Winning the War Within* (Nashville, TN: Thomas Nelson Publishers, 1988), p. 59.

Chapter 10: How a Habit Forms

1. Ed Silvoso, *That None Should Perish* (Ventura, CA: Regal Books Publishers, 1994), p. 154.
2. Kay Arthur, *Lord, I Need Grace to Make It* (Portland, OR: Multnomah Press, 1993), p. 12.

Chapter 11: You're Alive!

1. Charles Mylander in *A Way of Escape* by Neil T. Anderson (Eugene, OR: Harvest House Publishers, 1994).
2. Adapted from *A Way of Escape* by Neil T. Anderson, pp. 143-151.

Chapter 12: Choosing to Believe the Truth

1. Kay Arthur, *Lord, I Need Grace to Make It* (Portland, OR: Multnomah Press, 1993), p. 136.

Chapter 13: Steps to Freedom in Christ

1. Gordon McDonald, *Rebuilding Your Broken World* (Nashville, TN: Oliver Nelson, 1988), p. 153.

Chapter 14: Living Free and Staying Free

1. Charles Colson, *Loving God* (Grand Rapids, MI: Zondervan Publishers, 1987), p. 131.

Other Books by Neil and Dave

Awesome God
Bondage Breaker, Youth Edition
Bondage Breaker, Youth Edition Study Guide
Busting Free, Youth Curriculum
Extreme Faith
Reality Check
Stomping Out the Darkness
Stomping Out the Darkness, Study Guide
Ultimate Love

Other Youth Resources from Freedom in Christ

To My Dear Slimeball
by Rich Miller

Know Him, No Fear
by Rich Miller and Neil Anderson

Freedom in Christ Youth Conferences

Stomping Out the Darkness
For high school and junior high students

Setting Your Youth Free
For adults who serve youth

Purity Under Pressure
For high school and junior high students

For information about having a Freedom in Christ youth event in your area, call or write:

Freedom in Christ Youth Ministries
491 E. Lambert Road
La Habra, CA 90631
562-691-9128 Office
562-691-4035 Fax
www.ficm.org
info@ficm.org